ALCO LOCOMOTIVES

BRIAN SOLOMON

Voyageur Press

Dedication
To everyone at Genesee Valley Transportation for keeping the Alco spirit alive.

First published in 2009 by MBI Publishing Company and Voyageur Press, an imprint of MBI Publishing Company, 400 First Avenue North, Suite 300, Minneapolis, MN 55401 USA

The information in this book is true and complete to the best of our knowledge. All recommendations are made without any guarantee on the part of the author or Publisher, who also disclaims any liability incurred in connection with the use of this data or specific details.

We recognize, further, that some words, model names, and designations mentioned herein are the property of the trademark holder. We use them for identification purposes only. This is not an official publication.

Voyageur Press titles are also available at discounts in bulk quantity for industrial or sales-promotional use. For details write to Special Sales Manager at MBI Publishing Company, 400 First Avenue North, Suite 300, Minneapolis, MN 55401 USA.

To find out more about our books, visit us online at www.voyageurpress.com.

Library of Congress Cataloging-in-Publication Data

Solomon, Brian, 1966-
  Alco locomotives / Brian Solomon. – 1st ed.
    p. cm.
  Includes bibliographical references and index.
  ISBN 978-0-7603-3338-9 (hb w/ jkt)
  1. Locomotives–United States–History. 2. American Locomotive Company–History. I. Title.
  TJ603.3.A453S65 2009
  625.260973–dc22
                    2009009923

Front cover: Owned by the National Railroad Museum in Green Bay, Milwaukee Road No. 261 is a powerful Northern-type built during World War II, when the War Production Board limited diesel production, encouraging railroads to acquire new steam power instead. *Brian Solomon*

Frontis: Alco builder's plate and stack on Valley Railroad Locomotive No. 40, a 2-8-2 built in 1920 by Brooks Locomotive Works for the Portland, Astoria & Pacific. *Brian Solomon*

Title pages: The Century series was Alco's final locomotive line, introduced in 1963. Three Delaware & Hudson C-628s leading a southward freight approach the Mohawk River Bridge at Glenville, New York. *Jim Shaughnessy*

Table of contents: On the morning of July 19, 1992, Union Pacific Challenger No. 3985 reflects the clear Sierra sun at Portola, California, as it is readied for its westbound run over the former Western Pacific route through Feather River Canyon. UP and Alco worked together on the Challenger design, and UP ultimately operated the largest fleet. *Brian Solomon*

Back cover: On New Year's Eve 1957, a westward Mohawk Division local freight led by New York Central FA No. 1098 drops cars on the Fonda, Johnstown & Gloversville interchange. Working on the left in the distance is one of the FJ&G's two Alco S-2 switchers that will take the cars to Gloversville. *Jim Shaughnessy*

Acquisitions Editor: Dennis Pernu
Designer: Simon Larkin

Printed in China

CONTENTS

ACKNOWLEDGMENTS

The inspiration for this book began in the mists of my early childhood. Back in 1972, my father, Richard Jay Solomon, brought me to Penn Central's Beacon Park Yard in Boston, where we were invited into the yard tower. Although just five, I made one of my early photographs there, a black-and-white Instamatic image of an S-2 drilling the west end of the yard; I still have the negatives. About 10 years later, my mother, Maureen Solomon, was kind enough to write an elusively worded note to the administration of Monson Jr.-Sr. High School excusing my absence in order to photograph Duluth, Winnipeg & Pacific RS-11s on the southward Central Vermont road freight, which were expected to arrive in nearby Palmer, Massachusetts. I spent a pleasant afternoon waiting with my prewar Leica 3a for the freight to arrive, and my photographic efforts from that adventure are passable.

By that time, I was well acquainted with the CV's RS-11s, most of which had come to the railroad via fellow Canadian National U.S. subsidiary the DW&P, but this most recent batch was new to me. Although I'd made numerous other jaunts trackside looking for trains, these events contributed to my personal affinity for Alco locomotives. I'd be doing the reader a disservice if I didn't admit my partiality to the RS-11.

Robert A. Buck of Tucker's Hobbies in Warren, Massachusetts, deserves a great deal of credit for my early interest. In more recent times, he has offered his personal recollections of Alco steam and diesel power on the Boston & Albany and New York Central, as well as Central Vermont Railway, Maine Central, and New Haven. Bob described the thrill of watching DL109s pass at speed on the Shoreline. In addition, he generously loaned a number of photos from his collection. In the 1940s, Bob communicated with chief mechanical engineer S. Miller at Alco, who provided him with many prized builder's photographs. This kindness of more than 60 years ago says a lot about the dedication and passion of Alco's employees. Bob's son, Kenneth Buck, provided several interesting images of

Opposite: On November 28, 1946, New Haven Railroad two-cylinder 4-8-2 No. 3345 passed Sherborn, Massachusetts, leading a 60-car freight northward toward Framingham. This R-1-b class Mountain was built by Schenectady in 1924, essentially from the USRA standard plan. It was a real contrast with nonstandard 4-8-2s built for the New Haven in 1926 and 1928 that combined Alco's three-cylinder system with the unusual McClennon water-tube firebox and curious cast smokebox. *Robert A. Buck*

New York Central Alcos from the collection of Bob's friend, Warren St. George.

Doug Eisele of Genesee Valley Transportation is an old friend with whom I've shared railroad interest. In addition to lending me photographs, books, and his collection of *Extra 2200 South* magazines, he has opened many doors at GVT and contributed to my understanding of Alco diesels.

During the picture research for this book, I scoured dozens of collections and reviewed countless thousands of images. Kurt Bell and Nick Zmijewski at the Railroad Museum of Pennsylvania archive were exceptionally helpful in locating images of key Alco locomotives. Jay Williams of Indianapolis was also very generous with his historic collection. Jim Shaughnessy, whom I consider one of America's finest railway photographers, provided a wonderful selection of Alco's steam and diesel locomotives in action. Special thanks to Bondurant T. French and Paul Wussow for help with C. Richard Neumiller's excellent vintage photographs. John Gruber of the Center for Railroad Photography & Art in Madison, Wisconsin, helped locate images and provided a loan of negatives from Leo King's collection. Leo assisted with the captioning of his images. A number of other very fine photographers participated in this project, and their images are credited appropriately. All deserve credit for taking the time to seek out Alco locomotives and for allowing me to review their photos. The volume and quality of material received for this book was truly impressive. Readers would be astounded if they saw the photos I had to reject for no other reason than lack of space.

I've spent many months researching and reading about Alco, its engineers, and its locomotives. Thanks to the Irish Railway Record Society in Dublin for unrestricted access to its extensive library. My father maintains a substantial library of railroad literature, and this was crucial in all stages of my work. Pat Yough, Tim Doherty, and Tom Kline were among those who lent me materials for research. Special thanks to George S. Pitarys, Bill Linley, Tom Carver,

Hal Reiser, Pat Yough, Chris Southwell, Tom Hoover, Michael L. Gardner, Doug Moore, John Peters, Norman Yellin, Paul Goewy, Brandon Delaney, Sean Graham-White, Mike Abalos, Don Marson, and Brian Jennison for accompanying me (and often leading the way) on trips to photograph and inspect Alco and MLW diesels over the last two decades. I've spoken to many people who have worked on and with Alco diesels. Thanks to GVT's Matt Wronski for his interviews and insight. Tom Carver provided a variety of perspectives on Alco Centuries, a topic he has been researching for years. Bob Bentley of the Massachusetts Central provided a better understanding of the challenges of running a railroad with Alcos.

I've consulted many works while writing the text and captions. Among the books I found most interesting and most informative are: John H. White Jr.'s books on locomotives and locomotive builders; Alfred W. Bruce's *The Steam Locomotive in America*; Frank M. Swengel's *The American Steam Locomotive*; Albert J. Churella's *From Steam to Diesel*; John B. Garmany's *Southern Pacific Dieselization*; John Kirkland's *The Diesel Builders* series; the various diesel spotter's guides authored by Jerry Pinkepank and Louis A. Marre; and Richard T. Steinbrenner's epic. Of the magazines and journals, articles in Angus Sinclair's *Railway & Locomotive Engineering*, as well as news reports, articles, and commentary in *Railway Mechanical Engineer*, *Railway Age*, *Diesel Railway Traction*, *Trains*, *Railfan & Railroad*, and *Extra 2200 South* proved essential reading.

I hope my enthusiasm for Alco transcends these pages. I've tried to condense and distill a tremendous volume of information into a concise and interesting book, while keeping facts straight and details accurate. The fact remains, however, that it is not possible to cover, or even touch upon, all of the tens of thousands of locomotives built by Alco within this book. A great deal more could yet be written.

Enjoy!

INTRODUCTION

The American Locomotive Company was formed in 1901. It was known for most of its existence by the acronym of its initials—Alco (sometimes spelled ALCo). From 1956, the company formally adopted this acronym and became known officially as Alco Products. In the 68 years Alco was in business, it was a respected builder of locomotives. Its production spanned several significant transitions in American locomotive development and application.

In its early days, Alco participated in the transition from the relatively small and inefficient saturated-steam locomotives of the turn of the twentieth century to more powerful and more efficient machines characterized by superheated steam, large boilers, and radial trailing trucks. Likewise, it contributed improvements in steam-engine efficiency in the 1920s and 1930s, and it produced some of the largest reciprocating steam locomotives in the world.

Alco participated in the commercial development of the first successful diesel-electrics, emerging as a pioneer seller of diesel-electric switchers while continuing in its traditional role as America's second-most-productive steam locomotive manufacturer. Alco, with General Electric (GE) as its partner, emerged from the World War II economy as one of the leading producers of diesel-electric locomotives. Its partnership with GE ended in 1953, but of the three big steam manufacturers (including Baldwin and Lima), only Alco survived the steam-to-diesel transition. In the late 1950s and early 1960s, it survived the first rounds of the horsepower war, constructing high-horsepower replacement diesels. Alco had been in decline for some time at this stage, however. It faltered in the high-horsepower market and finally exited the business, although its Canadian affiliate, Montreal Locomotive Works (MLW), continued as a minor player in the business for another decade.

In the steam era, Alco's engineers were among the most talented, forward thinking, and innovative in the industry. Alco's technological development and locomotives cannot be effectively appreciated by considering Alco in a vacuum. The company was created as a reaction to competitive forces; this competition drove Alco's innovations and production. In the steam era, its primary competitor was Baldwin—historically America's largest steam locomotive manufacturer. In the 1920s, Lima emerged as an innovative player in the heavy steam market and competed with Alco and Baldwin in the lucrative road-locomotive trade. During the 1930s, General Motors' (GM) Electro-Motive Corporation (EMC; later its Electro-Motive Division, or EMD) developed modern, high-output diesel-electric locomotives and, in the course of a decade, redefined and dominated American locomotive production. In Alco's later years, GM largely defined the new locomotive market, style of production, and the basic types of locomotives sold. With the notable exception of the road-switcher, Alco's road diesels largely followed GM's patterns.

Alco can be credited for the first application, or pioneering development, of many significant technological advances in both steam and diesel technology. Alco's engineers looked beyond the immediate market for inspiration and innovation, paying especially close attention to developments in Europe. Alco's 0-6-6-0 compound of 1904 adapted and established the European-designed Mallet compound for use as a heavy North American freight locomotive. This design not only introduced the large articulated locomotive to the market but reintroduced the innovative Walschaerts valve gear and pioneered use of the power reverse lever, all of which were significant and lasting innovations. Alco was among the pioneers of superheating equipment and experimented with this energy-saving technology in the early years of the twentieth century.

Alco continually pushed the limits of locomotive design. Although it did not originate the wheel arrangements, in 1902 Alco effectively introduced the 4-6-2 Pacific as a large passenger locomotive, and two years later it helped pioneer the 2-8-2 as a heavy road locomotive. These two types would become the most successful passenger and freight types of the twentieth century. Alco built a Super Pacific as its 50,000th locomotive, demonstrating the capability of this wheel arrangement. Alco introduced the 4-8-2 Mountain type in 1911 and adapted the wheel arrangement for a powerful, fast freight locomotive for New York Central, known as a "Mohawk." It built some of the largest Mallet types ever conceived, notably massive 2-10-10-2s for coal service on the Virginian Railway.

During the 1920s, Alco reacted to demands for more powerful locomotive designs while providing innovative solutions for improved efficiency. Its three-cylinder simple types were aimed at increasing pulling power and efficiency without dramatically increasing locomotive axle weight. Other changes outside the industry benefited Alco's designs, such as advances in metallurgy that allowed improved boiler designs that could handle higher operating pressures.

The introduction of the two-axle radial trailing truck with Lima's 2-8-4 of 1924 led Alco to innovate several new types in the mid-1920s. In 1927, Alco helped engineer the first 4-6-4 Hudson for New York Central. That year, it collaborated with Northern Pacific (NP) on the pioneering 4-8-4 Northern, and a year later, Alco built an experimental 2-8-8-4 Yellowstone for NP. In the 1930s, Alco was responsible for the first new streamlined steam locomotives for the Milwaukee Road. Later, it built streamlined Hudsons for the Milwaukee that proved to be the fastest of their type, regularly operating at speeds in excess of 110 miles per hour. Alco's improved

On a crisp, clear February 18, 1996, the Chicago & North Western's Alco-built Ten-Wheeler No. 1385 works an excursion train on the Mid-Continent Railway Museum near North Freedom, Wisconsin. In its day, C&NW's R-1 4-6-0 was the most common locomotive on the railroad. Alco and Baldwin split the orders for C&NW's 325 R-1s. In steam days, it was common for railroads to divide orders between major builders. *Brian Solomon*

Hudsons for New York Central were considered among the finest steam locomotives on American rails. The manufacturer developed the 4-6-6-4 Challenger for Union Pacific (UP), a type credited as the first successful application of the articulated locomotive for relatively fast service. In 1941, it expanded the Challenger into the famous 4-8-8-4 Big Boy, one of the largest locomotives ever built. It ended the steam era with New York Central's magnificent 4-8-4, which the railroad referred to as the Niagara type.

Alco made several important contributions to diesel technology. It participated in the construction of the first commercially successful diesel-electric, although its partners engineered most of the significant innovations. In the late 1930s, Alco was the first American locomotive manufacturer to apply a turbo supercharger to increase engine output without a significant weight increase. In 1941, on request from Rock Island, it expanded and adapted the common switcher into a general-application road-switcher designed for freight and passenger service, road work, and yard work. This adaptation established a pattern that would later predominate.

Although Alco was involved in the pioneer production and sales of diesels, in the 1930s, its developments sagged behind those of General Motors. GM's flashy lightweight streamliners demonstrated the capabilities of new high-output diesels, which soon resulted in a whole line of very powerful and reliable locomotives. In 1940, Alco teamed up with GE in the construction of diesel-electrics. Alco was already playing catch-up in diesel development at this time, but it was still a leading producer of steam locomotives. GM's introduction of its very successful 567 engine, and its production passenger E-unit and model FT road freight diesel, led Alco to follow a similar course, yet its developments would largely fall on the heels of its competitor for the next three decades. At times, Alco would introduce a nominally more powerful model, but it was a step behind in terms of essential technological development and refinement. In the early 1940s, it reacted to GM's 567 engine with the development of its 241 diesel.

World War II interrupted and changed the course of locomotive development and production. Between 1942 and 1945, the War Production Board imposed limitations and restrictions on diesel locomotive production that tended to favor GM's road freight design. Although Alco continued to build diesel switchers, road-switchers, and steam during the war, its development of road diesels stalled. Alco's inadequate research and development during the war years, combined with high-level indecision about where to focus its resources, found the company even further behind GM when the war ended. With the market for diesels opening anew in 1945, Alco rushed to meet the competition. Although it sold thousands of locomotives during the steam-to-diesel transition and maintained its position as second-largest locomotive builder, Alco's diesels were not as well regarded as GM's. Design flaws led to reliability problems, which damaged Alco's reputation beyond repair. In 1953, its partnership with GE was dissolved. While Alco introduced improved diesels in the mid-1950s and 1960s, when GE separately entered the domestic market in competition with Alco and GM, Alco's fate was sealed. In 1968, it built its last locomotives, and in early 1969, it exited the U.S. market. In Canada, Alco's one-time subsidiary, MLW, continued to build locomotives derived from Alco's designs for a few more years.

While Alco was a significant exporter of steam and diesel locomotives, licensed its diesel-electric designs for construction around the world, built diesel engines for stationary and marine applications, and produced a variety of other machinery, the focus of this book is its North American locomotive production for domestic applications.

In 1925, brand-new Boston & Albany 4-6-2 Pacific No. 594 leads the eastbound Boston section of the *20th Century Limited* at Faneuil, Massachusetts. B&A Class K-6a 594, built by Brooks, lacks the elegance often associated with Alco designs. An air pump hangs indiscreetly on the front of the smokebox, giving the locomotive a lopsided appearance. Locomotives are not just about appearance, though, and the K-6 was a powerful machine with 75-inch drivers and 26x28-inch cylinders. *Photographer unknown, author collection*

CHAPTER ONE

EARLY STEAM POWER

Opposite: No. 50000 was a demonstration locomotive engineered by Alco's Francis Cole, a man celebrated for his advancement of locomotive technology. This was Cole's masterpiece and was designed for great, sustained power with maximum efficiency and low weight. It featured a host of innovations, including its recently introduced Schmidt superheater. Cole had studied the advantages of superheating since the early years of the twentieth century. The locomotive's road number was the same as its builder number, which symbolized the 50,000th locomotive built by Alco and its predecessors. *W. A. Lucas collection, Railroad Museum of Pennsylvania PHMC*

Eight of the best known commercial locomotive builders in the United States merged as American Locomotive Company in June 1901 in a joint effort to reduce competition between small producers and to more effectively compete with Baldwin, America's foremost locomotive manufacturer. Although this may seem an unusual mass consolidation of manufacturers, it was similar to other mergers and consistent with business-concentration practices at the time. (The same era saw the formation of U.S. Steel, General Electric, and several large railroad mergers. The trend ended with Teddy Roosevelt's trust-busting endeavors.) From its early days, the company was known by its abbreviation, "Alco," although this name wasn't formalized for many decades.

Alco's initial component companies consisted of: Dunkirk, New York–based Brooks Locomotive Works; The Cooke Locomotive and Machine Works of Paterson, New Jersey; Dickson Manufacturing Company of Scranton, Pennsylvania; Manchester Locomotive Works of Manchester, New Hampshire; Pittsburgh Locomotive and Car Works of Allegheny, Pennsylvania; Rhode Island Locomotive Works of Providence, Rhode Island; Richmond Locomotive and Machine Works of Richmond, Virginia; and the Schenectady Locomotive Works of Schenectady, New York. In order to build locomotives for the prosperous Canadian market, Alco acquired the recently formed Locomotive and Machine Company of Montreal Limited. Alco changed the name

An Alco builder's card displays New York, Ontario & Western 2-6-0 camelback No. 274, built by the Cooke works in June 1908. On the O&W these were known as "Mother Hubbards." Anthracite burners used the broad, shallow Wootten firebox to obtain a satisfactory fire and draft. *Thomas T. Taber collection, Railroad Museum of Pennsylvania PHMC*

of this affiliate to Montreal Locomotive Works in 1908. In 1905, Rogers Locomotive Works of Paterson, New Jersey, became the last major locomotive works to join Alco. In Alco's first few years, Cooke, Manchester, and Richmond were operated as subsidiaries before the company assumed full control.

Although it was a new name in locomotive manufacturing, Alco's component companies were well established, with solid reputations in the industry. The following are brief historical sketches of Alco's constituent works and how they related to the new Alco organization.

BROOKS LOCOMOTIVE WORKS

Founded in 1869 by Horatio G. Brooks, formerly an Erie Railroad master mechanic (and at the time, a superintendent of the line), and Marshall L. Hinman, Brooks Locomotive Works erected locomotives in the Erie's underutilized shop complex in Dunkirk. The Erie had been chartered to connect the New York City area with Lake Erie at Dunkirk, but after the Civil War, the railroad rapidly expanded and its main lines bypassed its once-important Lake Erie terminus. As a result, its shops there no longer represented strategic significance to the railroad. Although the Erie Railroad purchased from a variety of manufacturers, it remained a regular locomotive customer of Brooks until its inclusion in Alco. It continued to buy Alco products through the end of the steam era and was a large buyer of Alco diesels into the mid-1960s, by which time the Erie had merged into the Erie Lackawanna.

Brooks' engineering team was key to the early success of Alco. Alfred Bruce, Alco's later director of steam engineering, explained in his seminal book, *The Steam Locomotive in America*, that Brooks' Sherman Miller was later Alco's vice president of engineering, while Brooks' James G. Blunt coordinated Alco's draftsmen and remained active until the early diesel era. Brooks' mechanical engineer, John Player, served as a consulting engineer for Alco, while Brooks' plant superintendent, James McNaughton, moved on to become Alco's vice president of manufacturing.

THE COOKE LOCOMOTIVE AND MACHINE WORKS

One of four historical Paterson, New Jersey–based manufacturing companies that were involved in locomotive production in the nineteenth century, Cooke was founded in 1852 by Charles Danforth and John Cooke. Originally, it was known as Danforth, Cooke & Company. Previously, Danforth was a partner with Thomas Rogers, founder of the Rogers Locomotive Works (discussed later in this chapter). Like many locomotive manufacturers of the period, Danforth, Cooke & Co. was involved in the construction of a variety of heavy machinery. Locomotive production began in 1853. Following Danforth's retirement, the company changed its name to The Cooke Locomotive and Machine Works. In addition to locomotives, Cooke was the designated licensee for Leslie rotary snowplows. By using a small steam engine to spin vertical forward blades perpendicular to the tracks, these plows were capable of excavating tremendous volumes of snow, making them the most effective mechanized snow-removal device of the late nineteenth and early twentieth centuries. Alco continued to manufacture rotary plows at Cooke initially, but after it closed this plant in 1926, rotary production was shifted to other works.

NEW ENGLAND PLANTS

New England had been an early manufacturing center and, in the mid-nineteenth century, it was home to a variety of firms that built locomotives. Only two of these survived long enough to join Alco. Amoskeag, New Hampshire, was a mill town and manufacturing center that changed its name to Manchester in the 1830s. The old Amoskeag Manufacturing Company evolved over the years and produced a number of locomotives. At the end of 1877, the locomotive part of its business became known as the Manchester Locomotive Works. The company became a significantly more productive locomotive shop under Alco than it had been on its own.

Rhode Island Locomotive Works was the other New England locomotive builder to join Alco. This company had existed since 1861 and originated as a rifle builder for the Union armies. The Rhode Island Locomotive Works was among the smallest plants operated by Alco and was one of the first phased out of production, with the last locomotives built there in 1908.

DICKSON & COMPANY

Located in Scranton, Pennsylvania, Dickson & Company was formed by George, John, and Thomas Dickson in 1856. Following the acquisition of other industrial manufacturing businesses, it changed its name to the Dickson Manufacturing Company. In addition to steam locomotives and small locomotives operated by compressed air for use in mines and industry, the company also built railway cars and mining machinery. It was another of the smallest locomotive companies that joined Alco and was one of the earliest closed. Its last locomotives were built in 1909.

PITTSBURGH AND RICHMOND PLANTS

Andrew Carnegie was a partner in the Pittsburgh Locomotive and Car Works, a company formed at the end of the Civil War. It manufactured locomotives beginning in 1867 and expanded its facilities in the late 1880s and 1890s. Although the plant tended to produce switchers and other small locomotives that served the area's coal and steel industries, it was among the first plants capable of building the new large locomotives that were coming into vogue in the early twentieth century. Nonetheless, Alco closed the plant in 1919.

Metropolitan Iron Works of Richmond, Virginia, dated from the end of the Civil War. This manufacturing firm was expanded and became known as Tanner & Delaney. In *A Short History of American Locomotive Builders*, author John White found little to suggest the firm built locomotives before the late 1870s. The original premises were devastated by fire in 1883, leading to the construction of a new and more substantial plant. In 1887, the company changed its name to the Richmond Locomotive and Machine Works and emerged as one of the leading locomotive

Schenectady Locomotive Works was the most significant of Alco's component companies. Under the astute management of the Ellis family and the able engineering of Walter McQueen, Schenectady developed an excellent reputation in the nineteenth century. A classic example of Schenectady production is New York Central & Hudson River 4-4-0 No. 1022, built in 1892. Note the highly polished boiler plate as well as elegant steam and sand domes atop the boiler that characterized Schenectady designs. *Author collection*

manufacturers in the South. It was among the plants modernized by Alco, and it played a substantial role in mainline locomotive production until September 1927, when it was closed.

SCHENECTADY LOCOMOTIVE WORKS

Alco's largest and most significant predecessor was the Schenectady Locomotive Works, located in the upstate New York city of that name, a few miles northwest of the state capital at Albany. The company's origins dated back to 1848, when it was known as the Schenectady Locomotive Engine Manufactory, with connections to the Norris brothers of Philadelphia, and it was among the earliest commercial locomotive builders in the United States. Schenectady took its familiar name as result of reorganization in 1851. The following year, Walter McQueen joined the firm and helped build its reputation as a locomotive producer by engineering a number of exceptional machines during the second half of the nineteenth century. Its 4-4-0s were among the best of that type.

Schenectady's Albert J. Pitkin was the mechanical engineer for the company in its final two decades, having worked for the Rhode Island Locomotive Works previously, and for Baldwin prior to that. He joined Schenectady in 1882 and was promoted rapidly. By 1897, he was the firm's vice president and the works' general manager. He was the second president of Alco, a post he held until his untimely death in 1905. Well liked and highly regarded among his peers,

The 4-4-2 Atlantic type was among the first successful designs to incorporate a rear radial trailing truck, which allowed for a much larger firebox and thus greater power. With large drivers, the Atlantic was built for speed. Boston & Maine J-1 class No. 3242 arrives at Springfield, Massachusetts, on April 12, 1934. It was one of 41 of the class built by Alco at Manchester and Schenectady between 1902 and 1909, and it featured 79-inch driving wheels. *Photo by Donald Shaw, Robert A. Buck collection*

both in the United States and abroad, Pitkin was among Alco's star engineers. A story of his visit to the German Krupp works in the November 1905 issue of *Railway and Locomotive Engineering* relates that as Pitkin was "waiting to be escorted about, one of the [Krupp] officials entered the waiting room . . . and exclaimed, 'Mr. Pitkin, I shall gladly show you about the works if you will tell me how to pronounce the name of that town you come from.'" Pitkin had expressed a fascination with locomotives from an early age, and his personal interest in European travel and technology undoubtedly contributed to Alco's adaptation of European designs for American applications.

Schenectady was to become Alco's most important plant. The facilities were significantly enlarged, and after the last of Alco's other works in the United States ended locomotive production in the late 1920s, it was Alco's sole surviving locomotive plant, except for Alco's Canadian subsidiary, Montreal Locomotive Works.

Chicago & North Western's Class E Pacific No. 1564 was built by Alco's Schenectady works in July 1911. The varnished wooden "cow-catcher" pilot was still a standard feature on road locomotives of the period. As built, this locomotive had 75-inch drivers, 25x28-inch cylinders, the boiler operated at 185 psi, and it weighed 154,500 pounds. It carries green flags and markers, which would have been used for the first or advanced section of a passenger train under timetable and train order rules. *Chicago & North Western Railway photo by Christie, author collection*

A NEW CENTURY AND A NEW COMPANY

Alco was created on the eve of one of the greatest periods of locomotive development and construction, and it played a key role in directing American locomotive evolution and design. Alfred Bruce explains that Alco "concentrated under one head all of the production talent of the constituent plants and made immediately available to the new firm a vast reservoir of skilled personnel unified under a single management." Alco quickly broke new ground in a number of areas and pushed the American locomotive to new proportions and levels of performance and reliability. Among Alco's achievements was a new level of standardization in an industry famous for distinctive designs.

This was an exciting time for the railroads and a dynamic period of locomotive production. The American railroads were in their golden age and had yet to reach peak mileage. Traffic had been growing steadily for decades and was setting new records for freight tonnage and passenger miles. In the last decades of the nineteenth century, advances in railroad technology improved safety and enabled the operation of much faster, longer, and heavier trains than had been possible a generation earlier. Specifically, the invention and perfection of the Westinghouse automatic air

brake had greatly improved train handling. First applied to passenger trains in the 1870s, and more gradually to freight equipment, by 1900 the automatic air brake was nearly standard on most American railway equipment. Initially viewed as a safety device and resisted by the railroads because of its high cost of implementation, the air brake was key to safe operation of passenger trains at speeds of 80 miles per hour or more and enabled the operation of significantly longer freight trains. The Janey automatic coupler and improved draft gear allowed railroads to operate more tonnage behind a single locomotive. The invention of automatic block signaling increased track capacity by allowing trains to safely follow more closely and at higher speeds. Advances in bridge design, cheap commercially produced steel, and the introduction of reinforced concrete allowed railroads to construct more substantial spans with significantly greater load-bearing ability at lower cost than ever before. The invention of the steel plate-girder bridge combined with prefabricated steel tower supports allowed cost-effective bridge construction on a wide scale in places where line construction had been deemed cost prohibitive previously.

Except for the recent development of the electric interurban railway, by 1901 most steam railroads were virtually free of competition from other modes of transportation. The automobile was regarded as a rich man's toy, as the unreliable nature of early autos and the poor condition of most roads precluded long-distance highway commerce. The age of the canal had nearly come to a close, and the airplane hadn't yet been invented.

During Alco's early years, American locomotive manufacturing reached its all-time production zenith. Bruce cites 1905 as the high-water mark for American locomotive construction. That year, he estimates that 6,300 locomotives were ordered in the United States, a volume that kept all of Alco's various plants busy filling orders. Later, as locomotive production declined, Alco began to consolidate its manufacturing and gradually ended full-scale locomotive production at all of its plants except Schenectady works and Montreal Locomotive Works. Some of its other plants survived for a while as subsidiary manufacturers of locomotive components and other machinery. The last of the subsidiaries to end locomotive production in the steam era was the Brooks works in 1928, although this plant continued to manufacture heavy machinery for a number of years. Alco focused production at its Schenectady facility, enlarging and modernizing this plant to better accommodate larger, late-era steam designs.

From its early years, Alco had diversified its manufacturing production. Between 1905 and 1913, it built automobiles and trucks. It variously built other types of heavy machinery, including war munitions during World Wars I and II. Efforts to diversify led it to acquire other manufacturing firms.

LOCOMOTIVE DESIGN AND CONSTRUCTION

The steam-era business of designing and constructing locomotives fostered close working relationships between individual railroads' master mechanics and locomotive manufacturers. In most circumstances, locomotive design, regardless of manufacturer or intended service, used the

Opposite: Delaware, Lackawanna & Western's new 4-6-0 camelback No. 1012 poses with its engineer. This was one of five of this class built by Schenectady in 1905. *Thomas T. Taber collection, Railroad Museum of Pennsylvania PHMC*

same essential principles and technology. The fundamental elements of the reciprocating steam locomotive had been established in England during the early nineteenth century, first successfully blended in Robert Stephenson's famous *Rocket* of 1829. This machine combined three key design elements: a horizontal multi-tubular fire-tube boiler; a forced draft from the cylinder exhaust to feed the fire; and direct connections between cylinders and driving wheels. Most successful road locomotives in use around the world are considered descendants of the *Rocket*.

American locomotives usually had their cylinders located at the front, with the smokestack directly above, powering two or more driving wheels. In America, locomotives built after 1850 tended to be outside-connected (meaning the drive rods connected outside the wheels, rather than inside), and the wheels rode outside the locomotive frame. By contrast, many early-nineteenth-century locomotives in Britain and elsewhere were inside-connected with outside frames. Within these basic parameters there were considerable design variations. Locomotive types were defined by wheel arrangement. Locomotive designers and builders used various types of boilers, fireboxes, valves, valve gears (the equipment used to control the output of the valves), and a multitude of appliances and other equipment to refine the different locomotive designs.

Typically, railroads ordered new locomotives for specific service on a specific route. Each design would reflect the amount of work the engine would experience, with considerations for top operating speed, the typical train's weight, and operating constraints of the route. Because each railroad line was built and maintained to different specifications, crucial determinations for locomotive dimensions, such as the loading gauge (height and width) and maximum axle weight, varied. Maximum gradient was an important consideration, as this affected the maximum engine speed and helped determine how hard the locomotive would need to work. Other considerations included the type(s) of fuel to be burned in the firebox, quality of water used in the boiler, and length of the run.

In the nineteenth century, locomotive designers used an empirical assessment to match the intended output with the intended service. The success of locomotive designs varied. It wasn't unusual for experimental designs to be constructed in small lots and then gradually refined. More scientific methods were not applied to locomotive design until the early twentieth century. In general, orders were kept relatively small, with railroads rarely ordering more than a dozen or so machines at a time. Railroads tended to be very conservative in their acquisition of new motive power, and major design changes—even new wheel arrangements—took years to gain acceptance.

Specific locomotive designs were rarely viewed as the domain of an individual locomotive manufacturer, and many railroads routinely divided orders among different builders. Yet, the builders were able to distinguish their services in other ways, often through manufacturing excellence, by perfecting an element of construction, or by refining appliances. There was plenty of room to fine-tune any locomotive design, even where the basic parameters of wheel arrangement, cylinder proportions, and boiler size had been established. Several of Alco's component works had developed distinguished reputations. For example, Schenectady was known for its

Central Vermont 2-8-0 No. 464 climbs with an extra freight at Smiths Bridge in Monson, Massachusetts. Working Stateline Hill's 1.27 percent grade makes for a good show. Notice the exhaust steam from the tender, which indicates the booster engine is working to give the locomotive extra tractive effort. *Robert A. Buck*

Central Vermont 4-4-0 No. 85 *E. H. Baker* was photographed on a large glass plate at White River Junction, Vermont. An 1883 product of the Rhode Island Locomotive Works in Providence, this engine is a typical New England–built 4-4-0 of the period. Based in Providence, the company was first known as Burnside Rifle Company and expanded from gun manufacture to locomotives after the Civil War. It was absorbed by Alco in 1901, at which time it had capacity to produce about 150 locomotives annually. *Author collection*

well-built machines, Brooks for its innovative engineering, and Rogers had made its mark in international sales.

Alco's locomotives were noted for their clean appearance. Great attention was given to the arrangement, location, and aesthetic balance of external appendages such as pipes, air reservoirs, and air pumps. One common element of many Alco locomotives built in its first few decades was the shape of the steam and sand domes, characterized by more gentle, compound curves, and with tapered sides that resembled military helmets. By contrast, domes on Baldwin locomotives tended to be squared off and utilitarian in appearance.

LOCOMOTIVES OF ALCO'S EARLY YEARS

Although there had been a few significant technological advances in the 1880s and 1890s, and the proportions of locomotives had grown dramatically in recent years, a handful of wheel arrangements still accounted for the bulk of Alco production. One of the most common types in service remained the American Standard, the 4-4-0, which had been built in large numbers over the previous half-century. Bruce estimated that there were more than 11,000 4-4-0s in service on American mainline steam railroads as late as 1904. No longer preferred for moving heavy freight, the 4-4-0 was still adequate for hauling most passenger trains, local way freights, and branch-line mixed trains, as well as doing some yard work. Only the 2-8-0 Consolidation type was more numerous; it had come into favor during the 1870s and 1880s and reigned as the standard freight locomotive of the period.

As with all wheel arrangements, Consolidations built in 1904 were substantially heavier and more powerful than those a generation earlier. Not far behind the 4-4-0 was the 4-6-0 Ten-Wheeler, which had been growing in favor as a heavy passenger locomotive and was a respected light-freight hauler. More than 9,000 4-6-0s were on the books in 1904, and the type remained popular. The 2-6-0 Mogul accounted for more than 5,200 machines and had been a standard freight locomotive, although it had been waning in popularity since the adoption of the 2-8-0. The other standard wheel arrangements operated in large numbers were 0-6-0 and 0-4-0 switchers.

Because virtually every railroad had its own specifications, it is not practical to provide descriptions of each and every type of locomotive produced by Alco's various works in this formative period. A few typical and noteworthy examples are described in the text that follows. The bulk of Alco's production was of ordinary work-a-day machines. Because most of these were not unusual in either their dimensions or wheel arrangements, they tended to get little mention in the trade press of the time, unlike the noteworthy and superlative machines that set new records and established new standards.

Radial Trailing Truck

Introduction of the radial trailing truck in the 1890s had enabled the development of a significantly larger firebox, because it was no longer limited by the space between the frames. Where few railroads had sampled 2-4-2s, the largest interest was in 4-4-2 Atlantic and 2-6-2 Prairie types,

which railroads were ordering in growing numbers in Alco's early years. The Atlantic was largely built with tall driving wheels for express passenger services, while the Prairie was initially built for heavy passenger service as well as fast freight service. Here, "fast freight" must be qualified, because the term is very much relative to the typical speed of freight trains at the time. In the early twentieth century, heavy drag freights, such as coal trains, typically slogged along at 10 to 12 miles per hour. By contrast, high-priority merchandise trains might have operated at speeds of 25 to 30 miles per hour—considered fast for a freight train. For these fast services, a Prairie with 63-inch driving wheels was state-of-the-art motive power, and it was certainly faster than the older, heavy 2-8-0s with 57-inch drivers preferred for drag freights.

Freight Power

Typical of Alco's freight locomotives were 45 2-8-0 Consolidations built by the Schenectady works for the Erie Railroad during 1903 and 1904. The Erie had long established the 2-8-0 as its standard freight hauler, and the locomotives of this latest batch were classed H-20. Some of the Erie's earlier 2-8-0s were anthracite burners in the camelback configuration, and it had sampled various compound 2-8-0s in the early years of the twentieth century, but the H-20s were bituminous-burning simple locomotives and, in many respects, were just ordinary heavy freight machines. The boilers operated at 200 psi, drivers were 62 inches in diameter, and cylinders were 22x32 inches (diameter and stroke). Total engine weight was 202,000 pounds, of which 179,000 pounds was on drivers, and the locomotives were rated at 42,500 pounds tractive effort.

Another classic example is Chicago & North Western's Class R-1 Ten-Wheeler. C&NW ordered 325 R-1s between 1901 and 1908. As with previous large orders, this was divided between the Schenectady Locomotive Works and Baldwin. They might seem small today, but C&NW's R-1s were relatively big locomotives when they were new. They were heavy enough to require the railroad to improve its older bridges to allow R-1s greater service territory. As originally constructed, the R-1s weighed 164,000 pounds—9.5 tons more than older Class R Ten-Wheelers. Tractive effort was indicated as 30,900 pounds, and boiler pressure was 200 psi—typical for a road locomotive of the period. Most R-1s were built with a traditional Stephenson valve gear, which was located between the locomotive drivers, but some later R-1s used a Walschaerts outside valve gear (which had come into vogue in North America after 1904). The R-1 was the most numerous of any steam locomotive class on the C&NW; many lasted in service into the 1950s, when they were finally displaced by diesels. Alco-built No. 1385 is among three of the type preserved. It operated for a number of years at North Freedom, Wisconsin, on the Mid-Continent Railway Museum.

Compounds

A compound engine offers increased efficiency through multiple use of steam. Compounding was viewed favorably as a method of producing greater power from a boiler of given size or as a means of reducing water and fuel consumption for equivalent work done. Almost all of the commercially

Consolidations were typical of heavy freight locomotives built by Alco in the early years of the twentieth century. While Alco tends to be remembered for its milestone locomotives and massive or unusual experimentals, common locomotives such as this 2-8-0 represented the majority of its production. *W. A. Lucas collection, Railroad Museum of Pennsylvania PHMC*

Boston & Albany 4-6-0 tandem compound No. 221 was built by the Schenectady Locomotive Works in January 1899. The low-pressure cylinder on the right side (engineer's side) is 34x26 inches; on the opposite side is the high-pressure cylinder, measuring 22x26 inches. *Alco builder's card, Robert A. Buck collection*

built compound locomotives were double-expansion engines (two-stage expansion) in which steam exhausting from high-pressure cylinder(s) fed low-pressure cylinder(s) before exhausting into the atmosphere. A variety of nonarticulated compound arrangements came into vogue from the late 1880s and remained in production through about 1907, when the concept was largely abandoned as result of advances in superheating. Compounding found favor in Europe before it was adapted to North American practice. Alco's predecessors were instrumental in the introduction of compound locomotives in the United States. At Schenectady, Albert Pitkin refined an intercepting valve that allowed the engineer to switch from simple to compound operation at his discretion ("simple" is the term used to describe non-compound steam working).

Among the most common compound locomotives built by Alco were the cross compound and the tandem compound (first built by Brooks for Great Northern in 1892). Baldwin favored its patented four-cylinder Vauclain system and later a four-cylinder balanced compound design, but it built a fair number of tandem compounds as well, notably for the Santa Fe. Three-cylinder compounds enjoyed considerable success overseas but did not find favor in North America because of mechanical complexity and maintenance requirements.

Of the two types favored by Alco, the cross compound was a two-cylinder machine that featured a high-pressure cylinder on one side of the engine and a low-pressure cylinder on the other. The low-pressure cylinder needed to equal the power of the high-pressure cylinder, so it required a substantially larger diameter. This disproportionate cylinder arrangement gave cross compounds a decidedly unbalanced appearance.

Examples of this type were 2-8-0s built by Alco's Schenectady works for the Central Vermont Railway during 1904 and 1905. These were described in detail in the June 1905 issue of *Railway and Locomotive Engineering*. The high-pressure cylinder was on the left side and measured 22 1/2x32 inches (diameter and stroke); the low-pressure cylinder on the right measured 35x32 inches. Also significant to this locomotive were valve arrangements that were individually tailored to the different cylinders. The main valve on the high-pressure cylinder was a cylindrical, spool-shaped piston valve (a type coming into vogue during this period), while the low-pressure cylinder used a slide valve of the Allen-Richardson type. The locomotive used an indirect valve gear. Other than the boiler pressure, which at 210 psi was nominally higher than typical, other elements of this Consolidation were not especially unusual.

For starting, cross compounds used a special set of valves to allow the engineer to work the locomotive as a simple engine for short periods by directing high-pressure steam into both sets of cylinders. Sometimes described as starting valves, these allowed the locomotive to produce greater power than a normal compound but required a reducing valve to ensure equal piston thrusts from the different cylinders. While operating a compound locomotive as a simple engine gave a great amount of power, it voided the efficiencies inherent to the compound design, so railroads frowned upon such operation for any longer than necessary to get a heavy train in motion.

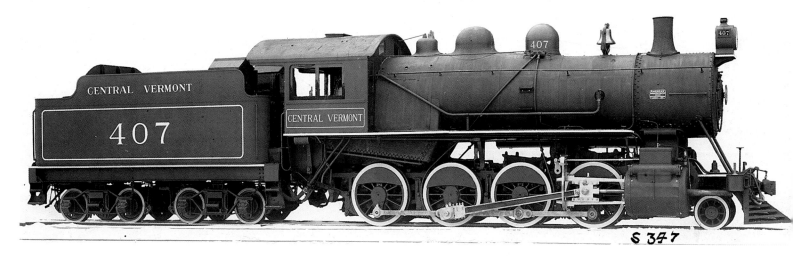

As one of the earliest commercially built compound designs, the cross compound had been built by the Schenectady, Pittsburgh, and Richmond works in the years prior to the Alco merger. It was favored by a number of railroads partial to compound designs. The type was free from complex valve arrangements and didn't require cranked axles or other troublesome equipment, and so it was considered the simplest and most straightforward of the compound designs. The design was not suited to high-speed services but to heavy, slow-speed freight service. As a result, the largest numbers of cross compounds were 2-8-0s, although a number of 4-8-0s, 4-6-0s, and 2-6-0s were also built. A few railroads ordered cross compounds for switching service. While compounds offered greater efficiency, engineers did not always view the locomotives favorably. On the Boston & Albany, the cross compounds were known as "slam-bangs," reflecting the uneven ride caused by motion from the high- and low-pressure cylinders.

The four-cylinder tandem compound was refined by Alco's Brooks works in the early 1890s. It featured a pair of cylinders on each side of the locomotive, with a high-pressure cylinder directly ahead of a low-pressure cylinder, connected to a common piston rod. One piston valve on each side of the engine controlled steam admissions for both high- and low-pressure cylinders. This type offered a more even thrust than the cross compound. In service, it was viewed more favorably, while the use of common crosshead and piston rods was found to be superior to more complex arrangements used by other four-cylinder compounds.

Like the cross compounds, tandem compounds were largely built as heavy freight haulers. They suffered from several problems, as noted by Frank M. Swengel in *The American Steam Locomotive*. Difficulties tended to develop in the packing between the high- and low-pressure cylinders. Maintenance was more complicated, because in order to access the low-pressure cylinder, it was necessary to remove the high-pressure assembly. The greater reciprocating weight of the four-cylinder, arrangement caused difficulties in counterbalancing, which was a problem at higher speeds. As a result, most tandem compounds were acquired for slower-speed services. Among the most enthusiastic buyer of the tandem compound was the Santa Fe, which embraced compounding with unusual fervor, acquiring a great many compounds of all types.

Despite nominal improvements in efficiency, higher maintenance costs and other limitations precluded the compound from universal adoption in the United States. Bruce estimated that in 1904 only 2,884 locomotives, roughly 6 percent of the national total, had been built as compounds. That year marked the introduction of the articulated Mallet compound, discussed in great detail later in this chapter. While the Mallet arrangements became the most popular of all the compound types, the nonarticulated two- and four-cylinder compounds fell out of favor.

The application of compound locomotives remained a controversial topic among locomotive managers. The means of operating them to their greatest advantage in terms of service and efficiency warranted much discussion in the railroad trade press. Take the comments of George H. Webb, divisional engineer of the Michigan Central, quoted in the October 1903 issue of *Railway and Locomotive Engineering:*

> *The fact that many of the roads operating compound engines are not having the success which they expected need not be laid entirely on the door of the locomotive engineer. If he is not doing as well as he should do, in a great measure the failure rests upon the traveling engineer, the road foreman of engines and the master mechanic as well. The engineer, if he is to do good service, must be educated.*

Despite the advantages of compounds, they rapidly fell out of favor in the early years of the twentieth century largely because of the practical development of superheating, which achieved much of the same efficiency of compounding without complicated equipment. Few nonarticulated compounds were built by Alco or other manufacturers in the United States after 1907.

Furthermore, many locomotives built as compounds were converted to simple operation after just a few years of service.

BIGGER LOCOMOTIVES

The development of the 4-6-2 as a heavy passenger-service locomotive was a significant milestone. This wheel arrangement had been tried several times since the 1880s, but it wasn't until 1902, when Alco's Brooks works built an order for the Missouri Pacific (MP) using a wide firebox supported by a radial trailing truck, that the 4-6-2 was established as a modern type. Designed for heavy mainline passenger services, it was named the Pacific type, acknowledging the MP's pioneer application. The Pacific was a logical expansion of the 4-6-0 and 4-4-2 types previously used in

passenger service. Furthermore, the type offered a solution to stability problems associated with the 2-6-2 Prairies when worked at speed. The Pacific's large boiler capacity, six coupled drivers, and four-wheel leading truck gave it a nearly perfect equipment combination for American passenger services. Soon after the MP's order, the Chesapeake & Ohio bought 4-6-2s with nearly identical characteristics. The type was rapidly accepted as a mainline passenger locomotive, becoming the most common passenger locomotive until the advent of diesel-electric road locomotives in the 1930s.

Contributing to the success of the 4-6-2 was the rapid increase in the weight of passenger trains combined with the desire for greater train speeds. The 4-4-2 Atlantic had demonstrated great speed potential but was not well suited to the heavier trains of the early twentieth century. Not only were passenger trains longer as a result of rising ridership, but train consists were more likely to include dining cars as well as head-end mail and express traffic. In addition, substantial weight

Baltimore & Ohio No. 2400 was America's first Mallet compound and set several important precedents for later development. In 1904, it awed onlookers at the Louisiana Purchase Exposition with its exceptional size, and it impressed students of locomotive technology because of its innovative accomplishments. Unlike many experimentals, No. 2400 enjoyed a long service life and wasn't retired from service until the late 1930s. Unfortunately, this pioneer machine was scrapped. *Thomas T. Taber collection, Railroad Museum of Pennsylvania PHMC*

increases resulted from the switch to all-steel cars during the first two decades of the century. Wooden equipment was phased out in reaction to several horrific disasters that demonstrated the dangers of wooden carbodies. Not only were wooden cars susceptible to fire, but also they tended to telescope (one carbody sliding over another) when trains crashed at speed or collided with one another.

New York Central adopted the Pacifics very early. It used them initially to better accommodate growing passenger business on its famed Water Level Route between New York and Chicago. The Central was known for very fast running and adopted the 4-6-2 to take advantage of its power and speed potential. A decade earlier, the Central had made world news with Schenectady-built 4-4-0 No. 999. On May 10, 1893, it set what was accepted as a world speed record of 112.5 miles per hour (an unlikely figure that is disputed today). Alco's Schenectady works constructed the Central's first five Pacifics in 1903. The Central designated these its Class Kg, and this remarkably handsome design featured a large, well-proportioned boiler with an enormous firebox for the time. The locomotives weighed 218,000 pounds, with 140,500 pounds on driving wheels providing 28,500 pounds tractive effort. Working pressure was 200 psi, and the driving wheels were 75 inches in diameter, with 22x28-inch cylinders. These locomotives saw the pioneer application of Alco's Cole trailing truck, designed by Francis J. Cole, one of the company's most influential engineers. The Cole truck became the standard for more than a decade. This Pacific's design included cast-steel main frames that, according to the May 1904 issue of *Railway and Locomotive Engineering*, featured "strong lateral bracing." Like most later Pacific types, drive rods connected to the second set of driving wheels. Significantly, the locomotive used piston valves instead of the standard slide valves, yet it still used an inside valve gear of the Stephenson type. Thus the Central's early Pacifics were a transitional design; within a few years, both outside valve gears and piston valves would become the standard.

Pacifics were built widely in North America. Many of the finest examples of the type were either Alco products or inspired by Alco. In 1911, Alco built a Super Pacific that it granted No. 50000—intended to reflect the 50,000th locomotive to roll forth from Alco's various works, a number including the production of its predecessor companies. This demonstration locomotive set forward a number of modern innovations. Significantly, it influenced the design of Pennsylvania Railroad's K4s Pacific, considered by many to be the finest example of the type.

Alco's Schenectady works pushed freight locomotives to new proportions. In 1901, it built a massive 2-10-0 tandem compound for the Santa Fe that *Railway and Locomotive Engineering* boasted was, "The largest and most powerful locomotive in the world." The engine weighed 259,800 pounds and rode on a 28-foot, 11-inch wheelbase. Although big for its day, this locomotive was soon eclipsed by much a larger machine.

OLD MAUDE: THE FIRST AMERICAN MALLET

In the early years of the twentieth century, a handful of American locomotive designers actively followed European locomotive technology, resulting in an infusion of European ideas. The application and adaptation of European technology to American locomotive design had significant long-term effects on American steam-locomotive development.

By 1901, Pennsylvania Railroad (PRR) owned and controlled its one-time rival, the Baltimore & Ohio (B&O). To exert its influence, and to direct the B&O's affairs, the PRR appointed one of its more progressive officers, Leonor F. Loree, as president of the B&O. A man of ideas and action, Loree was applauded for many physical improvements to the B&O initiated under his helm, including new freight yards and cutoffs to improve the flow of traffic. In 1903, the PRR, New York Central, and B&O moved to acquire locomotives that utilized successful European technology that was not yet in use in the United States for road trials and public exhibition at the Louisiana Purchase Exposition in St. Louis the following year. The PRR imported a state-of-the-art DeGlehn compound with a 4-4-2 wheel arrangement—intended for economical, fast passenger service—from French builder Société Alsacienne de Construction Mécaniques, while New York Central worked with Alco to build a 4-4-2 that adapted the DeGlehn design. However, the B&O followed a different approach and looked to apply European technology to heavy freight work.

Two decades earlier, in France, Swiss inventor Anatole Mallet (pronounced mal-LAY) had patented a variety of compound locomotive distinguished by its articulated design, effectively placing two engines under a common boiler. Locomotives of this type had been successfully applied to narrow gauge lines in Europe, where tight curves precluded engines with long wheelbases but steep gradients demanded locomotives with greater tractive effort.

Loree had witnessed an imported articulated locomotive at work in Mexico and began studying various articulated locomotives, including the Mallet, which for decades had been used on narrow gauge lines in Europe. On Loree's instruction, the B&O's general superintendent of motive power, John E. Muhlfeld, worked with Alco's Schenectady works to adapt the Mallet for heavy freight service. The resulting technological hybrid was unlike anything that had operated on American rails before. In contrast to diminutive European Mallets, Alco's Mallet was the heaviest locomotive ever built, taking the American trend toward ever-larger locomotives to a new plateau. It was completed in spring 1904 as the B&O's No. 2400 and named the *J. E. Muhlfeld*.

This 0-6-6-0's proportions and statistics awed railroad men. It weighed 334,500 pounds, substantially more than the record-setting 2-10-0 tandem compound constructed for the Santa Fe three years earlier. Alco boasted in its Louisiana Purchase Exposition brochure (which described Alco's 12 locomotives on display), that the Mallet was the heaviest and most powerful locomotive ever built at that time. The Mallet's enormous boiler contained 436 tubes, each 21 feet long and 2 1/4 inches in diameter, giving the locomotive 5,366 square feet of heating surface, and worked at an operating pressure of 235 psi. Estimates at the time of delivery set its tractive effort at 70,000 pounds. Driving wheels were 56 inches in diameter. The rear set of drivers was powered by high-pressure cylinders measuring 20x32 inches, and these exhausted into the front, low-pressure cylinders, measuring 32x32 inches. The forward engine was on a hinged frame and supported the boiler with a sliding bearing surface, while flexible steam pipes connected the cylinders.

Although the front engine was articulated to give the enormous machine flexibility in curves, the lack of a front guiding truck limited forward operation at speed, indicating that from its conception, the B&O intended to use the locomotive as a rear-end helper rather than for leading freight trains.

The Louisiana Purchase Exposition of 1904 was a great public event in the history of locomotive and railway development in general. In many respects, it was the early twentieth-century equivalent of the famous British Rainhill trials of 1829, when Robert Stephenson's *Rocket* proved its merit as a steam engine. The fair was a celebration of America's Louisiana Purchase centennial and highlighted technological innovation. A number of new locomotive designs were built specifically to exhibit at the fair—several of which would never be duplicated. Of all the locomotives displayed, the Baltimore & Ohio No. 2400 Mallet attracted the most attention. Less noticed was New York Central No. 3000, the Alco-built balanced compound.

After its display in St. Louis, where it caught the attention of the public and railroaders alike, No. 2400 was put to work on the Sand Patch grade. The B&O's (now a CSX) main line is relatively level between Cherry Run, West Virginia, and Cumberland, Maryland. West of Cumberland, its routes split; the B&O's original line to the Ohio River crosses the Alleghenies by way of a series of steep mountain grades via Grafton, West Virginia, while the Chicago line heads northwest through the Cumberland Narrows and into Pennsylvania toward Pittsburgh over Sand Patch, which begins near the former Hyndman Tower. To the north of the Maryland–Pennsylvania state line, the railroad winds its way along Wills Creek toward the summit of the Alleghenies at Sand Patch, near Meyersdale. A long tunnel just east of the mountain summit makes the grade more difficult for heavy trains.

The west slope of Sand Patch is not as grueling as the east, but still can present a serious challenge to heavy eastbound trains. To expedite train movements over the grades west of Cumberland, the B&O regularly assigned helpers to heavy trains. It was here that No. 2400 earned its nickname, *Old Maude*, after a popular cartoon mule of the era. In tests, No. 2400 could march up Sand Patch with a 2,000-ton freight as easily as two of the B&O's heavy 2-8-0 Consolidations, a particularly remarkable feat because the Mallet climbed the hill using 30 percent less coal than the pairs of 2-8-0s.

Old Maude was well engineered and well built. The rapid acceptance and popularity of the Mallet type in the United States can be attributed to Muhlfeld and Alco's careful attention to detail. This first Mallet remained in service on the B&O for 30 years. The Mallet design was refined, and approximately 2,400 locomotives of this design, using a variety of wheel arrangements, were built for service on U.S. rails over a 45-year period.

Significantly, No. 2400 reintroduced the Walschaerts outside valve gear. Designed by Belgian engineer Egide Walschaerts, this valve gear had been used by European manufacturers for many years and tried experimentally in the United States, notably on the Mason bogie engines in 1876. After its successful application on No. 2400, Walschaerts valve gear was routinely applied to American locomotives. Both Alco and the B&O's Muhlfeld actively promoted Walschaerts gear, touting its benefits over Stephenson's inside gear. The greater accessibility of Walschaerts gear, plus lower motion stress and reduced wear, gave it decided advantages over older types of inside valve gears. Muhlfeld wrote in a paper delivered to the International Railway Congress in 1905 that, "A motion gear placed outside of the frames certainly has the advantage of accessibility and convenience for inspection, lubrication, repairs and cleaning. . . ." Over the next few years, the growing size of locomotives caused Stephenson's gear to fall out of favor rapidly, replaced largely by Walschaerts and other varieties of outside gear.

Also significant to No. 2400 was the application of the power reverse gear, necessary because of the engine's exceptional size to allow the engineer to adjust both sets of Walschaerts gear simultaneously. Alco was keen to promote this feature, which was gradually adopted as standard equipment on new locomotives and ultimately mandated for safety reasons. In a 1920 advertisement, Alco recalled its achievement:

> *In 1904 the American Locomotive Company built the first Mallet locomotive in the United States. This design included a power reverse gear. We have been building power reverse gears ever since.*
>
> *Our engineers have been carefully watching the development of reverse gears, and, as occasion warranted, have made changes in our product.*
>
> *Today we have an ALCO REVERSE GEAR which we believe is as mechanically perfect as it is possible to make.*

MIKADOS

The 2-8-2 Mikado type was introduced by Baldwin in the 1890s, initially sold as an export locomotive most famously to Japan, where the type got its name. (At the time, Gilbert & Sullivan's opera *The Mikado*, about the emperor of Japan, was popular.) In its early domestic applications, the 2-8-2 was used as a specialized wheel arrangement and was not intended for mainline applications.

In the early years of the twentieth century, Northern Pacific ordered the bulk of its locomotives from Alco and its predecessors. NP was among the first to apply the 2-8-2 arrangement as a heavy mainline freight locomotive, placing orders with Alco's Brooks works beginning in 1904. By 1907, NP had ordered 160 2-8-2s, some of which were built as tandem compounds, others as simple

Opposite: Boston & Albany's H-5-g Mikado was a 1915 product of Alco Brooks. On October 15, 1947, No. 1214 led a two-car local freight and caboose up the east slope of Washington Hill west of Middlefield, Massachusetts. *Robert A. Buck*

Northern Pacific was among the first to order 2-8-2 Mikados for road freight service. The most unusual were a small batch of Alco-built tandem compound 2-8-2s. On each side of this four-cylinder compound type was an arrangement using a high-pressure cylinder directly ahead of a low-pressure cylinder connected to a common piston rod. By 1910, the 2-8-2 had become a standard freight locomotive, but by that time, tandem compounds were out of favor. Even these locomotives were rebuilt as two-cylinder, simple (non-compound) engines. *Thomas T. Taber c ollection, Railroad Museum of Pennsylvania PHMC*

Chesapeake & Ohio's K-3a was among the heaviest Mikados built for any railroad, weighing 358,000 pounds in working order per Alco's specifications—order number R-368. Locomotive No. 2320 was built by Richmond in January 1926. Northern Pacific's pioneering 2-8-2s, built by Alco 21 years earlier, weighed nearly 50 tons less than the C&O's K-3a, at 259,000 pounds. By 1926, the 2-8-4 was catching orders that previously called for heavy 2-8-2s. *Alco builder's card, author collection*

engines. These were big freight locomotives, and while not as large as the B&O's No. 2400, they were certainly noteworthy. The compounds weighed 271,000 pounds, delivering 44,340 pounds tractive effort with 63-inch drivers and operating at 200 psi. Yet the 2-8-0 Consolidation remained the standard for heavy freight service. During the second decade of the twentieth century, the 2-8-2 emerged as the most popular standard freight type, and it ultimately became one of the most common steam locomotives built in the later steam era. The combination of a large firebox and eight coupled driving wheels gave the locomotive an excellent mix of high tractive effort and horsepower, with flexibility and axle loading suitable for most lines. Frank Swengel estimated that approximately 10,000 2-8-2s were built for domestic freight services.

MASSIVE MALLETS

While Alco introduced the Mallet compound to America, Baldwin was the first to adapt the type for road service, building 2-6-6-2s for James J. Hill's Great Northern in 1906. Guide wheels made the 2-6-6-2 well suited for road work, as was the 2-8-8-2 type that followed it. Many of the early road-service Mallets were Baldwin products, but Alco produced a number of noteworthy machines as well.

In 1906, the Erie Railroad ordered three massive 0-8-8-0s from Alco for use as helpers over Gulf Summit east of Susquehanna, Pennsylvania. These were truly behemoths, built in camelback configuration with massive Wootten fireboxes containing 100-square-foot grates designed to burn anthracite culm—coal-mine waste consisting of coal fines, coal dust, and coal slack—the fuel of choice for many railroads serving the anthracite region of eastern Pennsylvania. These

tipped the scales at 410,000 pounds, making them the latest locomotives to claim the title of the world's largest. High-pressure cylinders were 25x28 inches, low-pressure cylinders were 39x28 inches, and the boiler operated at 215 psi. These locomotives were designed to deliver 98,000 pounds tractive effort, although published statistics from later years indicated tractive effort was a slightly more conservative figure of 94,800 pounds. They were equipped with Walschaerts valve gears. The Delaware & Hudson (D&H) tested one of the Erie's Mallets and bought 13 similar locomotives from Alco between 1910 and 1912. These were built as end-cab machines rather than as camelbacks, as the drawbacks of separated cabs had made the unusual type undesirable.

During 1912 and 1913, Alco's Richmond works built six massive 2-8-8-2 Mallets for the Virginian Railway for heavy coal service on its Deepwater Division, where grades exceeded 2 percent. On this line, trains routinely exceeded 3,300 tons. The new 2-8-8-2s were built to work in pairs as pushers, with an older class of Mallet leading, to lift trains of more than 4,200 tons over the line. February 1913's *Railway and Locomotive Engineering* reported the new locomotives weighed 540,000 pounds, with 479,000 pounds on driving wheels and a total weight including tender of nearly 750,000 pounds. Driving wheels were 56 inches, high-pressure cylinders were

Erie's three 0-8-8-0 camelback Mallets were among the most distinctive locomotives of their era. *Railway & Locomotive Engineering* followed the progress of these mammoth machines, and Angus Sinclair, the publication's proprietor and lifelong locomotive student, was honored at the christening of the machine in 1907. Later, the type was officially named the Angus Articulated by Erie president Frederick D. Underwood. No. 2601 is pictured at Susquehanna, Pennsylvania, where it was based as a helper for trains moving over Gulf Summit. *W. A. Lucas collection, Railroad Museum of Pennsylvania PHMC*

28x32 inches, and low-pressure cylinders were 44x32 inches. Using a factor of adhesion of 4.17, tractive effort was estimated at 115,000 pounds.

Over the next few years, the Virginian continued to order massive Mallet types. Its Baldwin-built triplex type of 1916 set a weight record at 806,460 pounds but were not deemed successful. By comparison, the 10 2-10-10-2s built by Alco's Schenectady works in 1918 were very successful. Numbered in the 800 class, each weighed 684,000 pounds and featured 30x32-inch high-pressure cylinders and absolutely gargantuan 48x32-inch low-pressure cylinders. Like most compounds, these could be operated as simple engines when starting, where they delivered 176,600 pounds tractive effort—the most of any reciprocating steam locomotive ever built. Working as compounds, their tractive effort of 147,200 pounds was still extremely impressive. Swengel wrote they were capable of hauling 17,050-ton coal trains from Victoria, Virginia, to the Virginian's tidewater coal docks at Sewells Point without the benefit of a helper.

Opposite: The Virginian's 2-10-10-2 Mallet tipped the scales with 617,000 pounds on the drivers. From the pilot to the back of the cab, it measured 73 feet, 3 inches. The leading engine had a 29-foot, 1-inch wheelbase. Its low-pressure cylinders were 4 feet in diameter, the largest ever installed on a locomotive. *W. A. Lucas collection, Railroad Museum of Pennsylvania PHMC*

MOUNTAINS AND MOHAWKS

New York Central No. 6225 was the first of an order for five L-2d Mohawks built in October and November 1929 for service on its Big Four lines. Cylinders were 27x30 inches, driving wheels were 69 inches in diameter, and boiler pressure was 225 psi. The engine weighed 367,000 pounds in working order, with 247,000 pounds on driving wheels. The engine delivered 60,620 pounds tractive effort with an additional 12,400 pounds provided by the booster. Although the New York Central tested a pair of Mohawks converted to three-cylinder operation, it opted against the concept and instead ordered large numbers of conventional two-cylinder 4-8-2s. *Alco builder's card, author collection*

In 1911, the Chesapeake & Ohio (C&O) designed a new, heavy passenger locomotive that blended characteristics of the 2-8-2 Mikado with those of the heavy 4-6-2 Pacific, using the previously untried 4-8-2 wheel arrangement. The October 1911 issue of *Railway and Locomotive Engineering* reported the locomotives were specifically designed to maintain a minimum of 25 miles per hour moving a 600-ton passenger train on the C&O's mountain grades. Because of this service, the C&O's superintendent of motive power named the 4-8-2 the Mountain type. Alco's Richmond works built the first three for the C&O. Two were delivered in 1911 and a third in 1912, featuring very large boilers, 62-inch drive wheels, and 29x28-inch cylinders. They weighed 330,000 pounds and delivered 58,000 pounds tractive effort. The type caught the attention of other railroads and, within a few years, several lines were operating Alco-built 4-8-2s.

In 1916, New York Central developed the 4-8-2 not for passenger service but rather for fast freight work on its Water Level Route main line. On this route, the Mountain moniker seemed incongruous, so New York Central called its 4-8-2s "Mohawks" after the river that its lines followed west of Schenectady, where the first of the locomotives were built. Its earliest Mohawks, Class L1, represented a fairly large order completed both by Alco and Lima. These used 69-inch drivers and 28x28-inch cylinders, weighed 343,000 pounds, and were rated at 51,400 pounds tractive effort. Ultimately, New York Central would continue to advance the type, and by the

New York Central L3a No. 3022 pauses at Pittsfield, Massachusetts, with westbound passenger train No. 49 on September 12, 1948. This L3 class was built by Alco in 1940 and, like most Mohawks, had 69-inch drivers. The front coupler is lowered into the pilot, a standard safety precaution on many of the Central's modern steam designs.
Robert A. Buck

1940s, it had amassed the greatest number of 4-8-2s, some 600 in total. Most of these were built by Alco, although the last Mohawks were Lima products.

The 4-8-2s were relatively successful and widely adopted across the country, with railroads using them in both passenger and freight services. In the 1920s, Alco modified the Mountain type with a three-cylinder simple engine (see Chapter 2). Despite the advent of larger and more powerful locomotive types, the 4-8-2 continued to be built into the early diesel era. In 1946, Vermont's Rutland Railroad ordered four modern 4-8-2s from Alco's Schenectady works. These featured 73-inch driving wheels using lightweight Boxpok drivers and conservatively proportioned 26x30-inch cylinders. (In *The American Locomotive Company—A Centennial Remembrance*, author Richard T. Steinbrenner notes the name "Boxpok" was a contraction of "Box Spoke," reflecting the nature of the cast-steel design.) These worked both freight and passenger services and were the Rutland's final new steam. They served for less than a decade and were replaced by Alco diesel road-switchers.

UNITED STATES RAILROAD ADMINISTRATION TYPES

The United States Railroad Administration (USRA) was set up to run the American railroads during World War I. Among its achievements was establishing standard designs for locomotive production. Engineers from Alco and the other major builders worked to draft the 12 standard USRA designs. During 1918 and 1919, Alco built more than two-thirds of the 1,856 USRA-standard locomotives, of which the most common were light and heavy Mikado types. Both featured 63-inch drivers; the light Mikado had 26x30-inch cylinders, weighed 292,000 pounds, and delivered 54,700 pounds tractive effort, while the heavy Mikado had 27x32-inch cylinders, weighed 320,000 pounds, and delivered 60,000 pounds tractive effort. Alco built 312 of the light Mikados.

The USRA also designed standard 0-6-0 and 0-8-0 switchers, 2-6-6-2 and 2-8-8-2 Mallet compounds, both light and heavy 2-10-2 Santa Fe's, a 4-8-2, and light and heavy 4-6-2 Pacifics. After the USRA relinquished control of the railroads in 1920, many railroads quickly reverted to their time-honored practice of ordering custom-designed locomotives. A few railroads embraced USRA standardization. Among these was the Southern Railway. The finest of the Southern's locomotives was its widely acclaimed Ps-4 Pacific type, of which 64 were built, 54 of them by Alco. The last of these were built by Richmond in 1926 and were painted green with elegant gold trim for service on the *Crescent Limited* and other express passenger trains. The Ps-4 became one of the most viewed locomotives in America, not specifically for its distinguished service but because for decades locomotive No. 1401 has been the centerpiece display at the Smithsonian Institution's National Museum of American History in Washington, D.C.

Opposite: During World War I, the United States Railroad Administration operated American railroads and established a dozen standardized locomotive designs in an effort to overcome difficulties caused by widely disparate individualized locomotive fleets. This locomotive was one of 65 USRA 2-8-8-2s built by Alco in 1918 and 1919 largely for Norfolk &Western and the Virginian. It was one of eight that N&W sold to the Santa Fe during World War II for helper service on Raton Pass. *Photographer unknown, author collection*

In the mid-1920s, Lehigh Valley's experimental three-cylinder 4-8-2, No. 5000, demonstrated its capabilities in freight service. After initial tests in heavy service on the west end of the system in June 1924, it was assigned to high-priority milk trains, typically working No. 38 east and No. 21 west. Loaded trains typically consisted of 25 specially designed, insulated cars, and needed to maintain speeds of 50 to 55 miles per hour. *Railroad Museum of Pennsylvania PHMC*

CHAPTER TWO

MODERN STEAM POWER

THREE-CYLINDER LOCOMOTIVES

Opposite: Grand Trunk Western 4-8-4 No. 6325 was built by Alco for freight and passenger service. It was restored in 2001 by the Ohio Central, which operated it in excursion service on the former Pennsylvania Railroad Panhandle line. *Brian Solomon*

As early as 1913, Alco engineers had investigated the benefits of three-cylinder locomotive design, but it wasn't until 1922 that Alco built its first experimental three-cylinder. The concept aimed to improve the performance of the nonarticulated locomotive using a three-cylinder system inspired by European designs. Alco's application of a three-cylinder design with a high-capacity boiler made for an interesting and nominally successful chapter in American locomotive design, yet this part of locomotive history is often neglected in light of Lima's concurrent "superpower" innovations that had a much greater influence on overall locomotive design and application.

In Europe, three-cylinder locomotives had been largely built as compounds, but Alco used a simple design—the boiler directly supplied all cylinders with high-pressure steam. The essence of Alco's design used two outside cylinders connected to drive wheels in the conventional manner and piston valves actuated by Walschaerts outside valve gear; the middle cylinder was connected by an inside main rod to a cranked axle. While the middle cylinder also used a piston valve, its valve motion was obtained using the Gresley system that featured levers deriving motion from the outside valves and valve gear. On most of Alco's three-cylinder designs, the cranked axle powered the second set of drivers, although in some examples the third axle was powered.

Alco applied its three-cylinder system in an effort to overcome the physical limitations of the locomotive's reciprocating parts, which had nearly reached practical maximum stress. Dividing boiler output over three cylinders instead of two solved this problem. Another benefit was improved torque. On all conventional two-cylinder locomotives, pistons are double-acting, meaning steam acts upon the piston in both directions. This provides the engine with four power impulses for each revolution of the driving wheels. A three-cylinder locomotive has six impulses, and as a result of greater division between impulse points, the angle between the pulses is reduced, which allows for more uniform torque. This substantially increases tractive effort without a large increase in engine weight.

In the paper "Design of the Steam Locomotive," presented on November 12, 1924, to the St. Louis Railway Club, Alco's mechanical engineer, James G. Blunt, explained the advantages of the three-cylinder design, saying, "It straightens out the tractive force fluctuations for each driving wheel revolution, delivers more tractive force per pound of weight involved and reduces the dynamic effects on the rail." Among the other benefits Blunt cited: ". . .six exhausts per driving wheel revolution produce more even draft on the fire, enabling the use of larger exhaust nozzles, with less back pressure in the cylinders, resulting in still greater fuel economy."

Alco's initial experiment was the conversion of two New York Central Mohawks, Nos. 2568 and 2569, to three-cylinder operation in 1922 and 1924. In addition, a booster engine was added to the trailing truck, which nominally increased the weight of the locomotive while substantially increasing tractive effort. While the two Mohawks remained relative curiosities on the New York Central, which initially had little interest in advancing the three-cylinder concept, other railroads were intrigued.

Alco built an experimental three-cylinder 4-8-2 for Lehigh Valley (LV) in 1923, its No. 5000. This locomotive featured 69-inch driving wheels and 25x28-inch cylinders. The total engine weight was 369,000 pounds, of which 246,000 pounds was on driving wheels; using a factor of adhesion of 3.81 (torque characteristics of three-cylinder locomotives afforded a lower factor of adhesion than an equivalent two-cylinder machine), tractive effort was calculated at 64,700 pounds. Lehigh Valley tested No. 5000 in a variety of services. Reports in *Railway and Locomotive Engineering* tell of No. 5000's assignments to LV's Buffalo Division (which at that time ran west from Manchester to the yards at Tifft Street, sometimes called Tifft Farms, in Buffalo—slightly less than 94 miles). In one test, No. 5000 hauled 70 cars weighing 4,540 tons in 4 hours and 45 minutes. During another test, it moved 94 cars weighing 4,619 tons in just over five hours. These performances were substantially better than Lehigh Valley's 2-10-2s, locomotives known for power but not fast running.

Lehigh Valley went on to test No. 5000 on its more mountainous lines between Lehighton and Sayre, where its performance exceeded that of other types. It proved especially able in milk train service, where it hauled trains ranging between 19 and 25 loaded cars on expedited schedules. Lehigh Valley was sufficiently pleased with the locomotive to order an additional five

Delaware, Lackawanna & Western ordered two classes of three-cylinder 4-8-2s between 1925 and 1927. Five, numbered 1450 to 1454, were built for passenger service. No. 2205 was one of 35 built for freight service (Nos. 2201–2235). *Thomas T. Taber collection Railroad Museum of Pennsylvania PHMC*

in 1924. During the next few years, Alco actively promoted its three-cylinder design and built a number of locomotives, largely using the 4-8-2 wheel arrangement but also building a few Pacifics and Mikados.

The Delaware, Lackawanna & Western, like Lehigh Valley, connected the New York metro area with Buffalo via the eastern-Pennsylvania anthracite fields. It bought several fleets of three-cylinder 4-8-2s. In 1925, Alco's Brooks works delivered five of the type with 73-inch drivers designed for heavy passenger service. During 1926 and 1927, the Lackawanna bought 35 freight-service 4-8-2s with 63-inch drivers. These were variously used on fast freight and coal services.

In 1924, New Haven Railroad bought some three-cylinder 0-8-0 switchers. Later, it ordered 13 three-cylinder Mountain types intended for fast freight service between Boston and the large interchange yard at Maybrook, New York, west of the Hudson River. These 4-8-2s were equipped with two other unusual features: a McClennon water-tube firebox, and a one-piece, cast smokebox designed by the New Haven's mechanical engineer, W. L. Bean. The March 1928 issue of *Railway Mechanical Engineer* reported that these 4-8-2s weighed 379,000 pounds, placing 260,000 pounds on driving wheels, and, using an 85-percent cutoff, could deliver 71,000 pounds tractive effort. The article noted that "increased demand for expeditious handling of traffic on the New Haven has made greater speed in the movement of its freight essential," and cited that a intended design goal for the 4-8-2s was to be capable of hauling 100 loaded freight cars weighing up to 5,000 tons at passenger train speeds.

The two most distinctive applications of Alco's three-cylinder design were for Southern Pacific (SP) and Union Pacific. SP sought a locomotive with more power and greater speed than its 2-10-2 Decks (SP found it unpalatable to describe the 2-10-2 wheel arrangement using its common name, "Santa Fe," named for SP's primary competitor) or its ponderous, cab-ahead Mallet types. Working with Alco, SP designed a new type of locomotive with the 4-10-2 wheel arrangement. This was an expansion of the 2-10-2 type, using an extra lead axle to help support the additional weight of the middle cylinder. The design required an abnormally long wheelbase that was accommodated by using a lateral-motion adjuster designed by James G. Blunt for the driving box on the lead set of driving wheels.

SP's 4-10-2s featured 63 1/2-inch driving wheels, 25x32-inch outside cylinders, and a 25x28-inch inside cylinder, with the boiler operating at 225 psi. The total weight of the locomotive was 442,000 pounds, of which 316,000 were on drivers. Using a factor of adhesion of 3.75, tractive effort was calculated at 84,200 pounds; however, using a booster engine, the maximum tractive effort was 96,530 pounds. The January 1926 issue of *Railway and Locomotive Engineering* noted that maximum cutoff was just 70 percent, compared with the 85 to 90 percent typical of most locomotives of the period. Alfred Bruce noted that the locomotives performed well at 30 to 35 miles per hour, while *Railway and Locomotive Engineering* revealed that the 4-10-2s' performance was favorable in graded territory compared to SP's 2-10-2s. Initially, SP assigned the 4-10-2s to its Donner Pass crossing and its Siskiyou Line to Oregon. *Railway Mechanical Engineer* noted that the 4-10-2 wheel arrangement was known from the time of inception as the Southern Pacific type and on Union Pacific as the Overland type. The latter name referred to the Overland Route, which aptly described both SP's and Union Pacific's lines that the locomotives originally served. Interestingly, SP amassed the largest fleet of 4-10-2s, 49 in total.

Union Pacific crossed many miles of wide-open spaces and, by virtue of its historic routes, served as a primary east–west artery, ensuring healthy volumes of freight traffic. During the Roaring Twenties, UP's traffic was robust, and it sought bigger, more powerful locomotives to accommodate growth. In particular, UP looked to improve operations on its heavily traveled main line between Green River and Laramie, Wyoming. In 1925, UP ordered a single, experimental three-cylinder 4-10-2, No. 8000, from Alco at approximately the same time as SP's order for 4-10-2s. This locomotive was nominally lighter than SP's, weighing 405,000 pounds compared with SP's 442,000 pounds. Boiler pressure was slightly lower, just 210 psi, and the outside cylinders had

a 2-inch-shorter stroke. UP tested No. 8000 in heavy freight service with impressive results. The May 1926 issue of *Railway and Locomotive Engineering* reported that the 4-10-2 was capable of hauling "twenty per cent more tons in regular service, with an expenditure of sixteen per cent less fuel per thousand gross ton miles."

Impressed with No. 8000, UP ordered another nine 4-10-2s—largely assigned to service on its heavily graded Los Angeles & Salt Lake Route—and its mechanical engineers worked with Alco to expand the locomotive into an even larger three-cylinder type. The result was the construction of experimental locomotive No. 9000, featuring the 4-12-2 wheel arrangement. Alco delivered it in 1926, ahead of UP's production 4-10-2s. The two outside cylinders measured 27x32 inches, and its inside cylinder was 27x31 inches. No. 9000's cylinders and related openings were made from large steel castings, which *Railway and Locomotive Engineering* reported as the first such application on a three-cylinder locomotive. The right-hand and middle cylinders consisted of one large casting, with the left-hand cylinder and related openings being a separate casting bolted to it. The middle cylinder sloped from front to back at 9 1/2 degrees in order to better work the cranked axle. Total engine weight was 495,000 pounds, with 354,000 pounds on drivers. Maximum tractive effort was calculated to be 96,600 pounds. The firebox grate was 108.3 square feet.

The 4-12-2 type soon proved its merit as a heavy freight hauler. Pleased with No. 9000's performance, UP ordered another 87 of the type from Alco. Not only did this give Union Pacific the largest single order for any three-cylinder type, but UP's 9000 class were the only 12-coupled locomotives built in the United States and were known as the Union Pacific type. The type's 30-foot, 8-inch wheelbase was the longest ever applied to an American locomotive (other locomotives with 12 or more drivers were built as articulated types). To allow the 4-12-2s to negotiate tight curvature, Blunt's lateral-motion device was applied to the first and last driving axles. Design

Alco delivered Union Pacific No. 9000 on April 9, 1926. It was the first of UP's 4-12-2s and the largest adaptation of Alco's three-cylinder concept. Despite the 30-foot, 8-inch driving wheelbase—the longest ever used by an American locomotive—UP's 4-12-2s could negotiate 16-degree curves because of the flexibility afforded by James G. Blunt's lateral motion devices on key driving axles. *Alco builder's card, Robert A. Buck collection*

speed was 35 miles per hour, but the locomotives were routinely operated at 45 to 50 miles per hour. After the delivery of 4-6-6-4 Challengers (discussed later in this chapter) in the mid-1930s, the 9000s were assigned to UP's Nebraska main line, where many served until the mid-1950s. The original No. 9000 locomotive is preserved and displayed in Pomona, California.

Alco's three-cylinder types were generally considered to be well-designed locomotives. Yet the three-cylinder concept did not achieve widespread acceptance in the United States. Baldwin also built some notable three-cylinder types, and the best remembered is its unusual high-pressure experimental No. 60000, which was preserved and displayed at the Franklin Institute in Philadelphia. Lima's superpower types, using a two-axle radial trailing truck to support a large boiler and firebox, proved to be a better means of increasing locomotive output. Other improvements included the development of high-output simple articulated types by Alco and other builders. Three-cylinder locomotives were not built after 1930. Among the problems with the design were difficulties in accessing the middle cylinder, which increased maintenance costs. However, Alco's Bruce asserted that when three-cylinder locomotives were maintained by experienced crews and operated in dedicated services, they exhibited excellent performance. A few railroads rebuilt three-cylinder locomotives as two-cylinder machines to simplify maintenance, yet many operated them as designed until the end of steam.

With green flags flying, Union Pacific No. 9027 leads the first section of freight No. 25. UP's 4-12-2s were extremely powerful machines. This frontal image provides a good view of the Gresley valve gear arrangement used to actuate the valve for the central cylinder. The valve can be seen clearly on the left side of the engine adjacent to the valve for the left piston. *Union Pacific, Jay Williams collection*

HUDSONS

A large firebox supported by a four-wheel rear trailing truck was key to Lima's development of its superpower 2-8-4 Berkshire type of 1924 and the 2-10-4 Texas type introduced in 1925. The ability to construct a large, high-capacity boiler that could deliver great quantities of steam at high operating speeds was pivotal to the superpower concept. Where Lima had first applied this to freight power, Alco worked with railroads to develop new passenger types. First of these was the 4-6-4 type designed to meet New York Central's need for a faster and more powerful passenger locomotive.

In 1926, New York Central's top locomotive designer, Paul Kiefer, drafted the 4-6-4 principle by expanding upon the railroad's most modern 4-6-2 Pacific type. Kiefer and Alco's engineers worked together in the design of a powerful, fast locomotive. The all-important firebox capacity was roughly 20 percent greater than the Central's modern Pacific. Kiefer and New York Central designed the locomotive, intended to haul its premier passenger trains, to not only perform well but to look good, too. The 4-6-4 was given a well-proportioned and balanced appearance. This was described in the March 1927 issue of *Railway and Locomotive Engineering* as a "stream line," which in the mid-1920s had a different meaning than a decade later—the concept of applying streamlined shrouding was still a few years away. Yet, the Hudson's styling proved prophetic; the Central's 4-6-4 was not only used as the model for early locomotive streamlining but was the first locomotive to be properly shrouded (discussed later in this chapter).

Prototype 4-6-4, Class J-1a, No. 5200, was delivered on February 14, 1927, aptly named the Hudson type in reference to the mighty Hudson River, which the New York Central main line followed for some 125 miles between New York City and Albany, New York. By all accounts, this was a magnificent locomotive. It featured 79-inch drivers, 25x28-inch cylinders, an 81.5-square-foot firebox grate, and operated at 225-psi boiler pressure. It was 88 feet long including tender, and total engine and tender weight was 552,000 pounds. The engine alone weighed 343,000 pounds, with 182,000 pounds on driving wheels, which delivered 42,400 pounds tractive effort. The trailing truck booster engine supplied an additional 10,900 pounds tractive effort.

Alco's Hudson type, like Lima's Berkshire (first built for the Central's Boston & Albany subsidiary), used a variety of modern, energy-conserving appliances. Where other modern locomotives were

In 1928, Alco Schenectady delivered 10 2-10-4 Texas types to the Central Vermont Railway. The CV had recently entered the Canadian National fold and had been completely rebuilt north of Brattleboro following Vermont's great flood of November 1927. The CV's 2-10-4s shared qualities with big CN designs. They were the largest locomotives in New England and were not allowed south of Brattleboro. On June 21, 1952, 2-10-4 No. 708 leads a southward freight across the Rutland Railroad diamonds at Bellows Falls. *Jim Shaughnessy*

notorious for their immodest appearance, most of the Hudson's auxiliary plumbing, including an Elesco feed-water heater, was concealed beneath the boiler jacketing to satisfy aesthetic concerns. Equipment used on the Central's prototype Hudson included a number of Alco's own designs. The main driving boxes were described in *Railway and Locomotive Engineering* as "fitted with supplementary bearings on both sides below the center line of the axle and . . . held in position against shoulders on the lower edges of the cross brass by wedges."

The prototype Hudson was broken in by working freight services, and soon it was tested in premier passenger work hauling the Central's "Great Steel Fleet." It proved enormously successful, delivering significantly more power than the railroad's best Pacifics, as described by Alfred Bruce:

> *Just prior to the adoption of the 4-6-4 type, the New York Central had put into service some powerful 4-6-2-type engines that had the same sized cylinders and drivers and about 2 percent less adhesion. The 4-6-4-type wheel arrangement, however, permitted an increase of 12-1/2 percent in steam pressure, 12 percent in heating surface, 20 percent in grate area, and 28 percent in the firebox gross volume. Thus when exhaustive comparative road tests were made, it was found that the 4-6-4-type produced 24 percent more drawbar horsepower and a 26 percent higher speed than did the 4-6-2 type—and that was the whole answer.*

New York Central ordered a fleet of 205 Class J-1 Hudsons from Alco between 1927 and 1931. The later locomotives featured a variety of improvements: They used Baker valve gears instead of Walschaerts, employed cast-steel frames, and was equipped with larger tenders. In addition, a fleet of 20 Class J-2 Hudsons was built for service on the Boston & Albany. These used 75-inch drivers that were better suited to the B&A's grades. The first 10 were built by Alco, the second 10 by Lima.

Kiefer and Alco continued to refine New York Central's Hudson design and ultimately crafted the J-3a—one of the finest machines to work American rails. In his book, *A Practical Evaluation of Railroad Motive Power*, Kiefer explained his design philosophy: "It has been our endeavor for succeeding reciprocating steam designs steadily to decrease weight per horsepower developed and to increase the steam generating plant and drawbar pull capacities and over-all thermal efficiencies."

Refinements included reducing the cylinder diameter to 22 1/2 inches while increasing the stroke by 1 inch to 29 inches. Operating pressure of the boiler was raised to 275 psi. To limit the total weight of the locomotive, aluminum was used for running boards, cabs, and other nonessential equipment. Metallurgical advances were another key to improved performance, and new alloy steels were used for piston rods, main rods, and other reciprocating parts to reduce damaging reciprocating forces that are especially severe at higher speeds. Instead of

Opposite: Ten years after the original Hudson, New York Central and Alco refined the design to achieve better performance and reliability. Alco built 50 J-3a Hudsons in 1937 and 1938. These had 22 1/2x29-inch cylinders, 79-inch drivers, operated at 275 psi, and were equipped with Baker valve gear and Elesco feed-water heaters. New York Central J-3a No. 5418 leads a passenger train at Cleveland, Ohio, in the early 1950s. The Scullin disc drivers were used to reduce wheel weight.
J. Williams Vigrass

traditional spoked wheels, J-3 Hudsons used lightweight drivers, either Boxpok or Scullin disc. Timken roller bearings were employed on all wheels, including those on the tender. The combined improvement proved extremely effective—the J-3a was capable of 875 more horsepower than the J-1 and developed a maximum 4,725 horsepower at 75 miles per hour. Significantly, the J-3s used less coal and water than the J-1s, and exhibited exceptional reliability and service records. The J-3s regularly ran more than 20,000 miles per month in passenger service on the Water Level Route. New York Central originated the 4-6-4, perfected the type, and owned more than half of all the 4-6-4s in North America.

One of the most curious and certainly best remembered variations of the New York Central Hudson was the streamliner. This was streamlining in the classic art deco sense, consisting of stylized sheetmetal shrouds. Streamlining was originally conceived to use aerodynamics to reduce wind resistance. Later, streamlined efforts were intended primarily to make the locomotive appear sleek and modern. The Central's Hudson had more streamlined variations than any other American type.

Some of the earliest efforts at modern locomotive streamlining were the work of Norman Zapf, an engineering graduate student at the then Case School of Applied Science in Cleveland, Ohio. Donald J. Bush, author of *The Streamlined Decade*, explains that in the late 1920s, Zapf performed wind tunnel tests on a model of the J-1 Hudson to demonstrate reduced wind drag. This research didn't immediately produce a full-size streamlined Hudson. It was in December 1934, after the success of Electro-Motive–designed lightweight streamlined trains—Union Pacific's *Streamliner* and Burlington's *Zephyr*—that New York Central finally applied streamlined shrouds to a steam locomotive. Its J-1 Hudson No. 5344, named *Commodore Vanderbilt*, was the very first American streamlined steam engine; its shrouding resembled an upside-down bathtub and was designed for improved aerodynamics. Following this pioneer effort, the Central applied no less than three streamlined treatments to its Hudsons, largely aimed at making the locomotives appear more modern, in keeping with the styles of the times.

Most famous of the streamlined Hudsons was Henry Dreyfuss' classic treatment, initially applied to 10 new J-3a's in 1938. This effort coincided with the introduction of the new streamlined *20th Century Limited*. These sheetmetal treatments interfered with routine maintenance, and most shrouding was removed after a few years. Many observers were unaware that beneath the sheet metal of the Central's sleek streamliner was just an ordinary-looking Hudson.

The Hudson type didn't achieve the popularity of the Pacific type. Yet, several American railroads bought Alco-built 4-6-4s, notably the Nickel Plate Road (NKP), which received its first 4-6-4s just a few months after New York Central's prototype. The NKP's 4-6-4s featured significantly smaller drivers than New York Central's. The Delaware, Lackawanna & Western bought a small fleet of 4-6-4s in 1938. Perhaps best remembered after New York Central's were the Milwaukee Road's streamlined F-7 speedsters (covered in more detail later in this chapter).

The most famous of New York Central's Hudsons were the last 10 built as streamliners, featuring classic styling by Henry Dreyfuss. In addition, New York Central's first streamliner, Hudson No. 5344, which received wind-resistant shrouds in 1934, was re-streamlined with the Dreyfuss treatment in July 1939. Central No. 5450, one of the final J-3a streamliners built at Schenectady, pauses at Englewood, Illinois, on May 6, 1939. It features Scullin disc drivers; other J-3a Hudsons were built with Boxpok drive wheels. *Jay Williams collection*

Opposite: Some of the most famous of all the 4-6-4s were Canadian Pacific's Royal Hudsons, so named because members of this class hauled special trains carrying King George VI and Queen Elizabeth across Canada in 1939. Gilded crowns clearly identified these magnificent machines. *Richard Jay Solomon*

ROYAL HUDSONS

Canadian Pacific Railway adopted the 4-6-4 type in 1929 and ultimately operated the second-largest fleet in North America, which totaled 65 locomotives. These were designed by CPR's British-born Henry Blain Bowen, who was quoted posthumously in an article by James A. Brown and Omer Lavallée in August 1969's *Trains*: "The Hudson type possesses ample boiler capacity to ensure the maintenance of high sustained horsepower, larger-diameter driving wheels to permit traveling at high speeds, and good riding and guiding qualities."

CPR's final development of the type were semi-streamlined engines, of the later H-1 classes, built by Alco's Canadian subsidiary Montreal Locomotive Works between 1937 and 1940. By far CPR's most famous locomotives, these last 4-6-4s were called Royal Hudsons—named because Class H-1-d Nos. 2850 and 2852 hauled special trains carrying King George VI and Queen Elizabeth across Canada in 1939. To signify the importance of this duty, all of the Royal Hudsons, Classes H-1-c, H-1-d, and H-1-e, were decorated with an embossed royal crown.

NORTHERN PACIFIC TYPE

In 1926, the same year that New York Central worked with Alco to develop the Hudson, Northern Pacific engineering forces worked with Alco in development of the 4-8-4. Like the Central, NP needed a more powerful passenger locomotive to haul its heavy transcontinental limiteds, but it faced a special set of challenges. Not only did NP have prolonged 2.2-percent grades in Montana, but it wanted to burn Rosebud lignite, which required an abnormally large firebox. NP essentially adapted the 4-8-2 Mountain type for this purpose. In so doing, it required a twin-axle trailing truck to support the great weight of the firebox, resulting in the first application of the 4-8-4 wheel arrangement. The firebox was designed with a 115-square-foot firebox grate, 52.5 percent larger than that employed by New York Central's bituminous-burning L-2a Mohawk, built by Alco the same year. The May 1927 issue of *Railway Mechanical Engineer* explained that if there were a need to burn more conventional grades of coal, the 4-8-4's firebox could be shortened by installation of a temporary brick wall.

The locomotives featured 73-inch drivers—ideal for fast passenger work, yet well suited to mountain grades. They weighed 426,000 pounds, which kept them to a maximum of 65,000 pounds per axle—the limits of NP's mainline axle loading. Since NP's pioneering 4-8-4s were a specialty application, proportionally they were rather different than subsequent 4-8-4 designs: the boiler was significantly smaller and required an elongated, large smokebox. The firebox was equipped with unusually large ash pan to accommodate the high ash content of Rosebud lignite.

Alco delivered NP's first 4-8-4s in early 1927. NP designated them as Class A, numbering them in the 2600 block. Significantly, the new wheel arrangement was named the Northern Pacific type. This wheel arrangement soon proved the most popular of the new superpower designs, was adopted by a variety of railroads, and was constructed by all the commercial builders as well as some railroad shops. Yet the "Northern" moniker was not universally adopted. In fact, no other wheel arrangement generated as many different names as the 4-8-4.

Some railroads used them exclusively in passenger service, others bought them for heavy freight work, while a number of lines used them in general mainline services, working both passenger and freight as traffic demanded. Within a year of the 4-8-4's introduction, several other North American railroads adopted the type. Close on NP's heels were Alco-built 4-8-4s for Lackawanna. Intended for passenger service, these had 77-inch drivers. Lackawanna called them "Poconos," after the eastern Pennsylvania mountain range its line traversed. In 1929 and 1932, Alco built two orders of 4-8-4s for Lackawanna with 70-inch drivers for freight service, with a final order in 1934 featuring 74-inch drivers suited for either passenger or freight work. Lehigh Valley, which bought 4-8-4s from both Alco and Baldwin, called them "Wyomings" after the valley in northeastern Pennsylvania that it ran through.

Canadian National Railways (CNR) was another early 4-8-4 buyer. With its U.S. subsidiary, Grand Trunk Western, CNR ultimately became the largest owner of 4-8-4s, buying a variety of relatively lightweight versions of the type for general service across its lines. Initially, CNR called the 4-8-4s "Confederations," after the Canadian confederation process that formed the Dominion of Canada from the British North American colonies in the nineteenth century.

UNION PACIFIC 800 SERIES 4-8-4s

Late to develop the 4-8-4, Union Pacific first experimented with Electro-Motive–engineered, internal combustion–powered, lightweight passenger trains before it even considered the Northern type. In February 1934, UP debuted America's first streamlined passenger train, a Pullman-built three-car articulated originally known as the *Streamliner*, powered by a Winton distillate engine. Its success led Union Pacific to invest in a fleet of diesel-powered, streamlined, lightweight trains. By the time its first 4-8-4s were being drawn up, the diesel had made its mark on UP. Notwithstanding the prior diesels, UP aimed to develop a more powerful steam locomotive to accommodate its fast and heavy passenger trains, which internal combustion locomotives were still not capable of hauling effectively. While Electro-Motive diesels had demonstrated the ability to haul specially designed lightweight trains, the old school still looked to steam for the movement of heavy trains. UP worked with Alco to design a powerful Northern with high drivers. With this philosophy,

Alco-built Northern No. 844 was Union Pacific's last new steam locomotive. Although retained primarily for passenger excursions, in modern times it has also occasionally worked freight. In 1989, it leads a westward grain train at Cheyenne, Wyoming. Built for power and speed, No. 844 was among the finest 4-8-4s ever built. *Brian Solomon*

Union Pacific had good company in the West, as the Santa Fe and Southern Pacific had also developed powerful 4-8-4s, the former working with Baldwin, the latter with Lima.

Alco built 20 4-8-4s for UP in 1937, Nos. 800 to 819, Class FEF-1 (UP's class system generally implies the wheel arrangement, in this case: Four-Eight-Four). These had 77-inch drivers and 24 1/2x32-inch cylinders, and incorporated modern locomotive-design elements for improved efficiency and reduced maintenance, such as one-piece, cast-steel, integral bed frames; Boxpok drivers; Timken roller bearings on all axles; and valves equipped with needle bearings.

Satisfied with the type, UP ordered more 4-8-4s from Alco with an improved design. Class FEF-2 was delivered in 1939 and Class FEF-3 in 1944. Both of these classes were more refined and had impressive characteristics and performance. They are considered among the ultimate 4-8-4 locomotives and a tribute to Alco and Union Pacific's engineering. Like the early 800s, these locomotives rode on 80-inch drivers. They used slightly larger cylinders, 25x32 inches, a 100.2-square-foot firebox grate, and a boiler with an operating pressure of 300 psi. They weighed 478,640 pounds, with 270,300 pounds on drivers. (The last 10, numbered 835 to 844, were slightly heavier, weighing 490,700 pounds, although the reported weight on the drivers was the same.)

UP's 800s were fast, powerful engines, designed to run at a sustained 90 miles per hour hauling a 1,000-ton passenger train. They were counterbalanced for 110 miles per hour and were reported to have exceeded 100 miles per hour on occasion. It has been claimed that top speed was only limited by an engineer's nerve. Equally impressive was an exceptional 93 percent service availability, comparable with diesels of the period. UP's 800s regularly worked approximately 15,000 miles a month. The most famous of this type is UP No. 844, the last in the class—it escaped retirement and has operated nearly every year since it rolled out of Alco in 1944, and it remains active as of this writing. This locomotive has been called upon to move freight in the modern era on occasion and has hauled carload trains on UP's Nebraska main line at track speeds without straining.

HIAWATHA SPEEDSTERS

In 1935, Milwaukee Road developed its *Hiawatha* streamliner in response to the new, internal combustion–powered, lightweight trains built for Union Pacific and Burlington. Powered by Winton diesels, the UP and Burlington trains had set new speed records and sparked an era of railroad streamlining. The Milwaukee aimed to match this performance using refined conventional steam technology.

Rather than a Hudson or Northern, the Milwaukee settled on the otherwise-obsolete 4-4-2 Atlantic arrangement. Although the type had been out of favor for 20 years, it seemed to be the best solution for speed, as Atlantics had always been built for fast service. The Milwaukee's engineers worked with Alco in the design of the fast Atlantics. While these largely employed established designs, they exhibited several distinctive and noteworthy features. Significantly, they were the first newly built streamlined steam locomotives and the first conventionally designed

Opposite: Milwaukee Road A1 Atlantic No. 2 departs Chicago with the *Hiawatha.* Delivered in 1935, the A1s were the first streamlined steam locomotives built new. Although they featured an older wheel arrangement and Walschaerts valve gear, the A1 Atlantics were very modern machines: fireboxes were all-welded construction, driving wheels used Boxpok cast-steel centers, and driving axles were hollow to reduce weight. Instead of a fabricated bed, a cast-steel bed was used that incorporated integral cylinders, the saddle, and the main air reservoir. The main rods were forged from high-tensile nickel steel in I-sections. *Vernon Seaver, Jay Williams collection*

steam locomotives with an operating boiler pressure of 300 psi. In addition, they took advantage of recently developed refinements, including Boxpok cast-steel driving wheels (instead of traditional spoked wheels), SKF roller bearings on hollow main axles, lightweight alloyed steel reciprocating parts, and precision counterbalancing.

A detailed article in the June 19, 1935, issue of *Railway Mechanical Engineer* highlighted the new locomotive's specifications: cylinders were 19x28 inches and total engine weight was 280,000 pounds, with 140,000 pounds on drivers, 75,000 pounds on the leading truck, and 65,000 on the trailing truck. Height measured from the top of the smoke stack was 14 feet, 4 inches; width was 10 feet, 2 3/8 inches; driving wheelbase was 8 feet, 6 inches; total engine wheelbase was 37 feet, 7 inches; and the total length of the locomotive (not including tender) was 53 feet, 2 inches. At 84 inches diameter, the driving wheels were among the tallest used by any modern American steam locomotive. Piston valves and Walschaerts valve gear were used to regulate steam admission to the cylinders. The boiler was oil fired and had a straight-top design. The firebox was 132 1/16 x 75 3/16 inches, with a 69-square-foot grate.

As with most modern locomotives of the period, the Milwaukee's Atlantic utilized an integral cast-steel bed that included the cylinders (and back cylinder heads) and main air reservoir. According to Bruce, General Steel Casting Corporation had perfected the single-piece, cast-steel frame in 1925.

Innovations in metallurgy that allowed the inexpensive production of stronger alloyed steels contributed to much-improved locomotive design by lowering the weight of reciprocating parts. On the Milwaukee's Atlantics, pistons powered drive wheels using lightweight tandem main rods, which were forged in an I-section profile using high tensile–strength nickel steel. *Railway Mechanical Engineer* wrote that "the counterbalancing of the locomotive is such that the dynamic augment [damaging reciprocating forces] at the rail at a speed of 100 miles per hour is 10,800 lb. The total reciprocating weights on one side of the locomotive amount to 1,003 pounds, of which one third are balanced. The low dynamic augment is due in part to the care in design to keep the weights of reciprocating parts as low as possible and also to the greatly reduced overhang of the pin-borne weights due to the relatively narrow cylinder spread."

Unlike most Atlantics of the earlier period, which had main rods connected to the rear driving wheels, the main rods were connected to the forward driving wheels on the Milwaukee's Atlantics. Frank M. Swengel noted that this arrangement was made possible by situating the cylinders sufficiently forward to allow for "acceptable main rod angles." Designated as Class A, the first two Super Atlantics were delivered to the Milwaukee on May 5, 1935. Two more were built by Alco in 1936 and 1937. Initially, the Class A Atlantics were conceived to haul five- and six-car consists, but the Milwaukee's design philosophy anticipated traffic growth, thus it chose trainsets of locomotives with conventionally coupled cars rather than a fixed articulated trainset. As the new *Hiawatha* grew in popularity, the railroad adjusted the size of train accordingly.

The *Hiawatha*'s streamlined shrouds followed aerodynamic principles as applied to both New York Central's No. 5344 and the Burlington's shovel-nosed *Zephyr*. December 1935's

A CHICAGO BOUND STREAMLINER

A penny postcard from the late 1930s portrays the Milwaukee Road's A1 Atlantic No. 4 at the Wisconsin Dells racing the *Hiawatha* toward Chicago. No. 4 was the last of four high-speed streamlined 4-4-2s built for the 410-mile *Hiawatha* service between Chicago and the Twin Cities. The locomotives blended the older 4-4-2 wheel arrangement with a host of modern innovations. *Richard Jay Solomon collection*

Railway Mechanical Engineer reported that in the summer of 1934, Alco jointly conducted wind-tunnel tests at New York University with car builders American Car & Foundry and J. G. Brill to compare the wind resistance of various shapes and patterns. Although they were often introduced simultaneously, aerodynamics and streamlined styling are two different concepts. While the Milwaukee could have achieved less wind resistance with subtle styling, its inspiration for shrouding its Atlantics was as much in regard to public perception as its need to reduce wind resistance.

Much of the aerodynamic work was Alco's, while styling was credited to famed designer Otto Kuhler. Kuhler had been promoting locomotive streamlining for several years and had gained the attention of both Alco and the Milwaukee Road. Locomotives were styled to match new lightweight cars built for *Hiawatha* service. Both were decorated in a gray, orange, and maroon scheme that featured large, stylized, silver wings wrapped around the front of the locomotive. The shrouding was a steel frame mounted on the running boards that completely covered the top and sides of the boiler and extended down nearly 3 feet below the running boards to conceal the reverse gear, valve gear, and water pumps. The June 1935 issue of *Railway Mechanical Engineer* noted that for access to critical machinery for servicing and routine maintenance, "shrouding

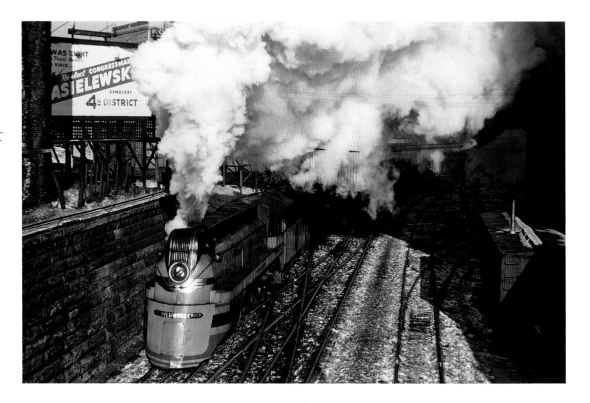

One of the Milwaukee Road's famous streamlined F-7 Hudsons blasts out of Milwaukee with a *Hiawatha* in 1943. These were the fastest steam locomotives in regular service in the United States. *James P. Schuman, Railroad Museum of Pennsylvania PHMC*

is fitted with doors opposite all washout plugs, sand traps, boiler checks, etc. The entire front is enclosed in swinging doors, the opening of which gives access to the front-end and the equipment mounted on the front deck."

The success of the Atlantics led the Milwaukee to work with Alco to design more powerful streamliners. In August 1938, Alco delivered six elegant streamlined Hudsons to the Milwaukee Road, designated as F-7s (not to be confused with the common Electro-Motive diesel-electric built between 1949 and 1954 that carried the "F7" designation). The F-7 embodied a streamlining treatment similar to the Class A Atlantics, but with a distinctive futuristic flair that was unlikely to be mistaken for anything else. The November 1938 issue of *Railway Mechanical Engineer* indicates this was the joint work of the Milwaukee's engineers, Alco, and Otto Kuhler. The F-7s used 84-inch-diameter, cast-steel Boxpok driving wheels, a General Steel Castings cast-steel bed with integral cylinders, back cylinder heads, air reservoirs, and other vital equipment. It used a Walschaerts valve gear and piston valves. Cylinders were 23 1/2x30 inches bore and stroke, while pistons were of the Z type, made from rolled steel. Piston rods were made from normalized and tempered medium-carbon steel, with multiple-bearing cross heads. Main rods and side rods were forged with low-carbon nickel steel. Total engine weight in working order was

For its operation of transcontinental passenger services with Union Pacific, Chicago & North Western ordered nine Alco-built Hudsons. Inspired by the Milwaukee's F-7 in 1938, C&NW designated its 4-6-4s as Class E-4. These exhibited a more subdued streamlining treatment than the Milwaukee's and were colored in the traditional Pullman green with elegant gold striping. The locomotive was 56 feet, 5 3/4 inches long; 10 feet, 10 3/4 inches wide; used 84-inch drivers and Baker valve gear; and weighed 412,000 pounds. *Robert B. Graham, Jay Williams collection*

415,000 pounds, of which 216,000 pounds was on driving wheels. The tender weighed 375,000 pounds in working order. Rated tractive force was 50,300 pounds. This compared with 43,440 pounds on New York Central's J-3a (engine output only, as the J-3a was equipped with a booster). While the Atlantics were strictly intended for Chicago–Twin Cities *Hiawatha* runs, the six Hudsons were expected to work a variety of long-haul passenger trains, including transcontinental services such as the *Olympian*, as far as Harlowton, Montana. On much of the Milwaukee Road (save for its electrified divisions), coal was the standard fuel.

Milwaukee streamliners routinely operated at speeds in excess of 100 miles per hour over extended runs to maintain the *Hiawatha*'s published schedule. It is claimed that they often hit speeds near 120 miles per hour, and on occasion may have traveled faster.

JUBILEE

In 1936, Alco's Montreal Locomotive Works built five semi-streamlined 4-4-4 Jubilee locomotives for Canadian Pacific Railway. These were near cousins to the Milwaukee's Class A Atlantics, with many technological similarities despite differences in styling and a different wheel arrangement. In common with the Class A Atlantics, CPR's 4-4-4s had a large firebox, used 300-psi boiler pressure, featured lightweight reciprocating parts and Boxpok drivers, and were intended to haul lightweight passenger cars.

CHALLENGERS

In 1928, Alco pushed the size envelope when it developed the 2-8-8-4 Yellowstone type for Northern Pacific. This enormous experimental was the first articulated type to use the four-wheel, load-bearing, trailing truck. Deemed the largest locomotive in the world when completed, it was specifically designed for NP's unusual operating needs on its Yellowstone district between Glendive, Montana, and Mandan, North Dakota. Here, it operated long heavy freights on a sawtooth gradient profile that was not conducive to helper operations. Complicating matters, NP wished to burn locally mined Rosebud lignite. As in the case of its 4-8-4s discussed earlier, low-yield coal required a larger firebox grate than comparable locomotives burning high-yield bituminous coals. NP's Yellowstone required a phenomenally large firebox—the largest on any locomotive ever built—that measured 22 feet long and 9 feet wide. Its exceptional weight necessitated a four-wheel trailing truck. The firebox grate was also the largest ever used, at 182 square feet. Although Alco's experimental 2-8-8-4 resulted in UP ordering 11 additional locomotives, production was awarded to Baldwin, which underbid Alco.

Typical of large, simple-articulated types, NP's Yellowstone was built for relatively slow-speed operations. While most simple articulateds of the 1920s were capable of faster operations than the older Mallet compounds, maximum speeds were rarely more than about 40 miles per hour. This changed in the mid-1930s, when Alco and Union Pacific worked together in the design of the

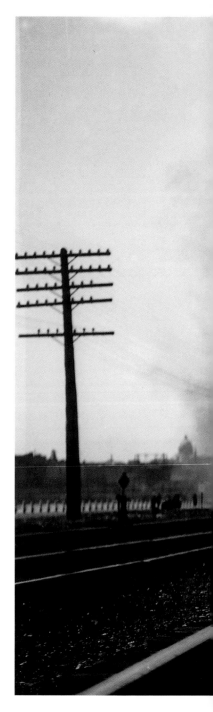

Union Pacific No. 3821 was built in 1937 as part of the railroad's second order for 25 Class CSA-2 Challengers. Where older articulated types were designed for heavy, slow-speed work, the 4-6-6-4 was built for speed and was capable of sustained operation up to 80 miles per hour. This was possible by ample boiler capacity, improved articulation, and a highly refined suspension system. Robert O. Hale—remembered as a master of the panned photograph—captured this Challenger at speed near Rawlins, Wyoming, about 1956. *Robert O. Hale, Jay Williams collection*

4-6-6-4 type aimed at much faster service. Union Pacific's interest in the 4-6-6-4 stemmed partially from the success of Alco's three-cylinder 4-12-2s designed in the late 1920s. Although a powerful type, the 4-12-2's long wheelbase limited its application.

In 1936, Alco delivered the first 4-6-6-4 articulateds to UP. They featured 69-inch drivers; 22x32-inch cylinders; weighed 566,000 pounds, of which 366,000 pounds was on drivers; and delivered 97,400 pounds tractive effort. Significantly, this type combined several innovations. Its four-wheel leading truck provided improved front-end stability. More even weight distribution between forward and rear engines allowed for better balance at higher speeds. These traits, combined with a high-capacity firebox and boiler, tall drivers, and great flexibility afforded by an articulated wheelbase, made for a powerful, adaptable locomotive designed for a maximum running speed of 80 miles per hour. Unlike the 4-12-2 that was limited by its long wheelbase and more moderate speed, a 4-6-6-4 could operate on most Union Pacific main lines and was well suited for both freight and passenger work. UP named the wheel arrangement the "Challenger" and ultimately ordered 105 of the type. Later Challengers were heavier and slightly more powerful.

Opposite: Union Pacific Challenger No. 3985 is one impressive machine; it measures more than 16 feet tall and is nearly 70 feet long (not including the gigantic centipede tender). Union Pacific and Alco worked together in the Challenger design, and UP was first to use the type and ultimately operated the largest fleet; No. 3985 was one of the last 25 Challengers built for the UP by Alco. On June 28, 1982, it worked east at Mt. Green, Utah. *George W. Kowanski*

The Challenger's articulation offered a significant improvement over earlier types and was based on what Alco described as the "lever principle." The locomotive also benefited from a well-engineered suspension that gave it flexibility where needed. A further innovation, introduced about 1940, was an improved lateral bearing surface supporting the forward engine, which minimized vertical movement and further improved ride quality. Of the Challenger, Bruce wrote, "The result is the most stable-riding articulated engine ever built."

Where the 4-12-2 was unique to UP, the Challenger type enjoyed considerable interest among other railroads. George Drury, in his *Guide to North American Steam Locomotives*, notes that 252 were built. While specifications varied, they were the most numerous simple-articulated type built in the United States. The majority of 4-6-6-4s were built by Alco, including those for the Clinchfield, Delaware & Hudson; Northern Pacific and its affiliated Spokane, Portland & Seattle; and Western Pacific. Baldwin built the type for the Western Maryland and the Rio Grande, while a handful of Alco Challengers built for the Rio Grande during World War II were later sold to the Clinchfield.

BIG BOY

In 1940, Union Pacific desired a locomotive with sufficient power to haul its fast, heavy, perishable trains east on its heavily graded route between Ogden, Utah, and Cheyenne, Wyoming. UP's fruit blocks were solid trains of agricultural produce that originated in California for transport to Eastern and Midwestern cities, and were among UP's fastest scheduled freights. While UP's ascent of the Wasatch east of Ogden is not as steep as the Donner Pass crossing of the Sierra, or Northern Pacific's transcon, or even its own lines to Los Angeles and Portland, the Wasatch was an extremely busy double-track line that required extra power.

Electro-Motive had just recently introduced its 5,400-horsepower model FT freight diesel, but rather than embrace the newfangled diesel—as had its competitor, the Santa Fe—UP worked with Alco to design the powerful 4-8-8-4 locomotive for the important task of moving fruit blocks.

Although UP had embraced diesel power for its lightweight passenger trains in the mid-1930s, it had developed a good working relationship with Alco. This resulted in the design of most of its successful locomotives, including its three-cylinder 4-12-2s, 800-class 4-8-4s, and 4-6-6-4 Challengers as described above.

The 4-8-8-4 design was in essence an expansion of the established 4-6-6-4 type. Although its driving wheels were an inch smaller, 68 inches in diameter, the locomotive was still impressive because of its exceptional length and weight. And although the locomotive and tender was 132 feet, 9 3/8 inches long, its design enabled it to accommodate curves as tight as 20 degrees. Engine weight was 772,000 pounds.

In August 1952's *Trains & Travel*, David P. Morgan relates the story of an Alco shop employee who scrawled "Big Boy" in chalk on the smokebox door of a 4-8-8-4 under construction. The name stuck and quickly brought fame to the massive machines. While often cited as the largest ever built, as it turned out, the Chesapeake & Ohio's massive 2-6-6-6 Alleghenies built later were slightly heavier—a little-known fact revealed long after the steam era had ended, and thus often overlooked by historians.

Big Boys were equipped with modern equipment, such as roller bearings on drivers and some reciprocating parts, while cylinders were integrally cast with the locomotive bed. Among the striking features of the locomotive were the enormous steam pipes from the boiler to the cylinders. Much larger than those on other articulated locomotives, these were designed for high capacity to give the locomotive maximum power. Although many UP steam locomotives were oil fired, the Big Boys were primarily coal burners.

The first Big Boy was delivered to Union Pacific at Council Bluffs, Iowa, on September 4, 1941, entering service a few days later to haul a freight train of more than 100 cars.

The 4-8-8-4 was designed for both power and speed and could easily reach 70 miles per hour, although 60 miles per hour was a more typical top speed in regular service. Its maximum output was developed at 30 miles per hour. The magnificent size and power of the Big Boy awed filmmakers, newspaper reporters, and authors. Lucius Beebe described the Big Boy in *Trains in Transition*: "Its boiler delivers 7,000 horsepower, it has a cruising speed of eighty miles an hour and consumes twelve tons of coal and 15,000 gallons of water every sixty minutes." Alfred Bruce estimated Big Boy's maximum output was closer to 7,500 horsepower. This was a far greater amount than Electro-Motive's FT, but the FT had greater starting ability and was a more flexible machine.

UP's Big Boys had a limited service territory because of their size. It was not that their axle loading was too great, or even that their wheelbase was too long for many UP main lines; what tended to limit the Big Boys' operation was that the locomotives were too large to fit on turntables and other servicing tracks. Because they were designed for a special application, the railroad had little incentive to reconfigure servicing facilities to expand the locomotives' territory. Typically, Big Boys worked as intended over UP's main line between Ogden and Cheyenne, and occasionally worked from Cheyenne to Denver.

Union Pacific only bought 25 Big Boys, built by Alco in two orders in 1941 and 1944. The Big Boys survived later than most steam locomotives, moving trains over Sherman Hill as late as 1958. Their enormous size has made them among the most famous American locomotives despite their relatively small numbers and obscure service. Today, eight of the locomotives are preserved around the country, some rather far from where they operated.

Opposite: A mechanic inspects the forward engine on Union Pacific Big Boy No. 4005 at Laramie, Wyoming, in July 1957. The Big Boy was created when Otto Jabelmann directed Union Pacific's research and mechanical standards department to work with Alco in the design of a locomotive capable of moving full-tonnage trains over the Wasatch east of Ogden without need for a helper. The first 20 4-8-8-4s were built in 1941, and an additional 5 came in 1944. The Big Boy's running gear was a design success that gave it flexibility in curves and a high level of rigidity on tangent track.
Jim Shaughnessy

MILWAUKEE ROAD S-CLASS 4-8-4s

The Milwaukee Road was among the first lines to adopt the 4-8-4. Its first class was the S-1s built by Baldwin in 1930. Ten years later, Baldwin delivered its S-2 class. Both types were largely intended for freight work. During World War II, the Milwaukee sought new power yet was faced with War Production Board's restrictions, and so needed to order compliant locomotives that did not require complicated new engineering or were solely for passenger work. Alco blended several existing 4-8-4 designs to come up with a dual-service (what the British would call a "mixed-traffic") locomotive. Ten were constructed between July and September 1944. Designated Class S-3, these had 26x32-inch cylinders and 4-inch Boxpok drivers. Total engine weight was 460,000 pounds. The S-3's operating pressure was 250 psi. As built, these were coal burners with a 96.6-foot grate, but in 1950 they were converted to oil burners.

After the end of steam operations, two of the ten were preserved. Most famous is No. 261, owned by the National Railroad Museum at Green Bay, Wisconsin, and restored to service by the North Star in 1993. In 15 years of excursion service, Milwaukee Road No. 261 was reported to have worked roughly 40,000 miles and carried more than 275,000 passengers while hauling excursions in 16 states from Montana to West Virginia and Kansas to New York. Significantly, it has done this without a major failure or mechanical breakdown. And yet it has often been accompanied by a less reliable diesel as both a back-up and sometimes to provide head-end electrical power to passenger cars. Today, it is among the favorite excursion locomotives in the United States and is featured on the cover of this book. As of this writing in early 2009, it was undergoing a second restoration to prolong its service life.

NIAGARAS

New York Central's 4-8-4 Niagara was the work of the Central's locomotive genius, Paul Kiefer. In 1930, the railroad had experimented with a unique Alco-built, high-pressure, three-cylinder compound with a 4-8-4 arrangement, but this locomotive had virtually no influence on the Central's later steam policy or its Niagara designs. Rather, the Niagara was a culmination of Kiefer's designs, effectively an enlargement of the successful L3 and L4 4-8-2 Mohawks that blended the technological refinements of the J-3 4-6-4 Hudson.

Unconvinced by the promise of diesel-electrics, Kiefer held to a belief in the capability of the steam locomotive. His design team worked with Alco to create a prototype 4-8-4 built for both high-speed passenger service and fast freight service. This was a difficult task because the powerful locomotive needed to conform to New York Central's unusually restrictive loading gauge, limiting it to 10 feet, 5 inches wide and 15 feet, 3 inches tall. To enable a larger boiler space within these confines, Kiefer dispensed with the conventional steam dome, instead employing a dry pipe for steam collection. The boiler design was considered one of the best, and its evaporative capacity was substantially more productive than the boiler of a typical 4-8-4.

Owned by the National Railroad Museum in Green Bay, Milwaukee Road No. 261 has operated in mainline steam excursion service for a number of years. This powerful Northern-type steam locomotive was built during World War II, when the War Production Board limited diesel production, encouraging railroads to acquire new steam power instead. Had it not been for the war, fewer lines would have purchased late-era steam power. *Brian Solomon*

Niagara No. 6000, Class S-1a, was completed by Alco in August 1945. Consistent with modern steam design, it had a cast-steel, integral bed frame. All wheels and reciprocating parts were equipped with Timken roller bearings. Lightweight alloy steel reciprocating parts were precision counterbalanced, and valve gear was of the Baker type. Boiler pressure was initially set at 275 psi and later raised to 290 psi. The firebox featured a 101-square-foot grate; cylinders were 25x32 inches. Main rods were manganese-vanadium steel. To keep weight down, non-operational parts, including the cab, running boards, and elephant-ear smoke lifters, were made from aluminum rather than steel. No. 6000 weighed 471,000 pounds with 275,000 pounds on the driving wheels. Initially, the locomotive was equipped with 75-inch drivers, but it was soon retrofitted with 79-inch drivers. It delivered 62,400 pounds maximum tractive effort and developed 6,600 maximum cylinder horsepower at 77 miles per hour, while maximum drawbar horsepower was 5,050 at 63 miles per hour. It could sustain an 18-car passenger train at 80 miles per hour.

Based on the success of the prototype, in 1945 and 1946, the Central ordered an additional 26 Niagaras—an unusually late date for a significant steam purchase. Twenty-five were Class S-1bs and largely resembled the prototype, but with lower operating pressure and slightly reduced tractive effort. All had 79-inch drivers and Baker valve gears. A sole Class S-2a was different than the rest; instead of more conventional piston valves and valve gear, it used experimental Franklin rotary cam–actuated poppet valves. The Central's Niagaras demonstrated extraordinary service and performance, averaging more than 25,000 miles a month. While they equaled diesel performance, they did so at much greater cost, which soon proved their undoing.

New York Central's Niagara has been considered one of finest steam locomotives ever built. This photo depicts No. 6000, Central's S-1a prototype. Its novel features included a significant use of aluminum alloys for the air pump shield, cab, dome castings, handrails, and smoke lifters, among other components. Potentially confusing to historians, the aluminum was provided by Pittsburgh-based Aluminum Company of America (ALCOA). *Alco builder's card, Robert A. Buck collection*

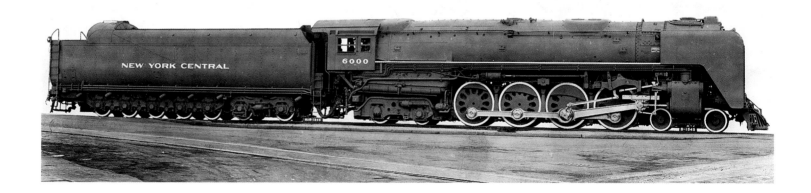

The New Haven Railroad routinely assigned rarely photographed DL109 pairs to road freights. Based on 25-percent adhesion, starting tractive effort for a pair was 117,500 pounds. The eastward ruling grade between Providence and Boston was 0.4 percent, and a pair of DL109s, such as these passing Providence about 1954, were rated to move 4,000 tons in a train of up to 100 cars. *Leo King, courtesy Center for Railroad Photography and Art*

CHAPTER THREE

EARLY DIESELS

Opposite: Reading Company No. 99 works street trackage in Philadelphia on June 24, 1947. This 300-horsepower Alco-GE-IR diesel switcher was completed in March 1928 as Reading No. 51. It was the first production boxcab equipped with this configuration of single roof-mounted radiator fan, and it was built three years after the pioneering Central Railroad of New Jersey No. 1000, the locomotive considered the first commercially successful diesel-electric. *J. R. Quinn collection*

In 1923, General Electric and engine manufacturer Ingersoll-Rand (IR) built an experimental prototype diesel-electric locomotive. It used GE electrical and mechanical components and was powered by IR's commercially successful diesel engine. Designated No. 8835, the locomotive came to life at Phillipsburg, Pennsylvania, on December 17, 1923. Its construction propitiously coincided with new legislation in New York City that expanded on earlier laws banning steam-locomotive operation within Manhattan by 1926. While most passenger operations had already been electrified because of those laws, some freight and switching operations had remained steam-powered; now the railroads needed to consider alternatives.

In June 1924, the diesel-electric prototype began a tour of 13 railway companies. Among those with the greatest interest in the locomotive were companies serving the New York/New Jersey waterfront, including the Baltimore & Ohio, Central Railroad of New Jersey, Lackawanna, Long Island Rail Road, New Haven, and New York Central. The diesel switcher was ideal for small yards along the waterfront, where electrification was neither practical nor cost effective.

Alco's early involvement with diesel-electrics was an outgrowth of its work with General Electric in the construction of heavy electric locomotives. The successful demonstration of No. 8835 led GE, Ingersoll-Rand, and Alco to join in a construction consortium. Alco supplied mechanical components (carbodies, running gear, and so on), as it had done for GE electric locomotives. GE was responsible for

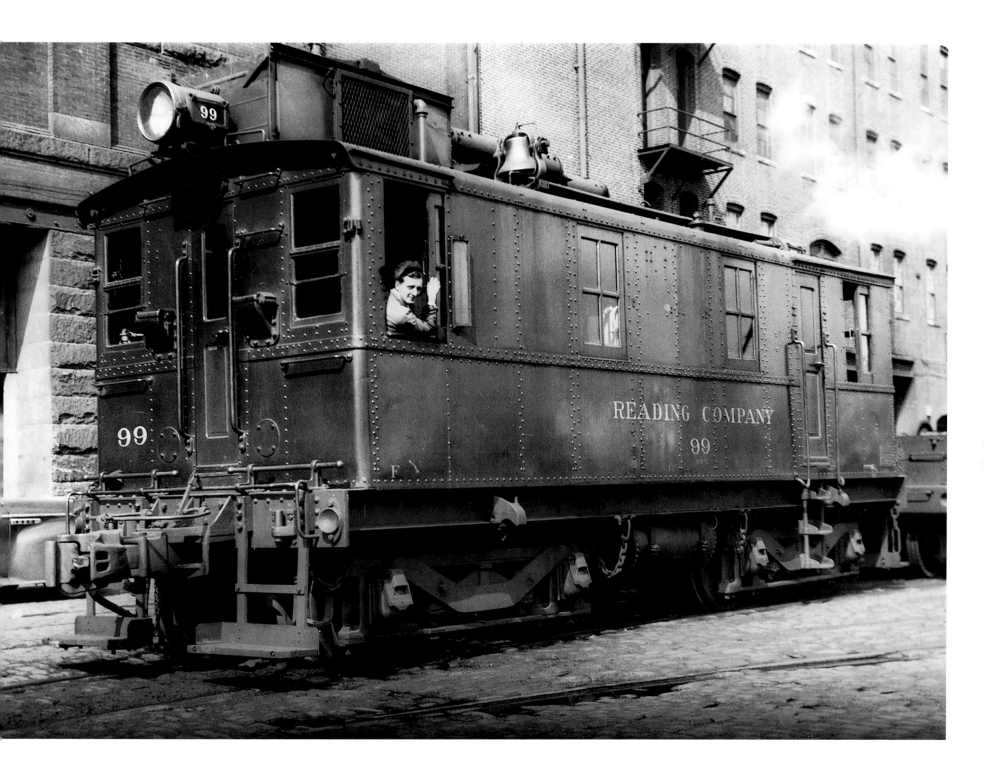

most of the engineering and supply of electrical components, while Ingersoll-Rand provided the diesel engine and handled marketing and sales.

Technologically, diesel-electrics were an outgrowth of electric locomotive and gas-electric railcar production. Neither Alco nor other manufacturers viewed these diesels a serious threat to big steam power. Diesel engine technology had not yet matured. Although functional and reliable enough for slow-speed switching applications, the existing engine designs had very high weight-to-power ratios; they were relatively large and heavy while producing low power. The IR engine developed only 300 horsepower.

The Alco-GE-IR consortium built 31 boxcab diesel-electrics between 1925 and 1928. The bulk of these diesels were bought for switching in Eastern cities, primarily in the New York region, where air-quality regulations were in effect. Central Railroad of New Jersey No. 1000 was the first locomotive sold from this demonstration effort, considered by many locomotive historians as the world's first

No. 301, Alco's first diesel-electric switcher with the end-cab design and the hood body style, was built in June 1931. It was powered with the McIntosh & Seymour model 330 diesel, rated at 300 horsepower. It had four GE-297A traction motors, and starting tractive effort was 39,600 pounds. Continuous tractive effort at 3.7 miles per hour was 19,040 pounds, and top speed was 40 miles per hour. The Alco builder's card indicates it was built for the Lehigh Valley, while Kirkland's *Dawn of the Diesel Age* explains it was constructed as a demonstrator and later sold to the LV, becoming No. 102. Alco built nine switchers similar to this; most went to the U.S. Navy. *Alco builder's card, Jay Williams collection*

New York's Jay Street Connecting Railroad operated a variety of historically significant diesels. No. 5 is one of the early Alco hood-style switchers powered by the 531 diesel, while No. 300 is Alco's very first production diesel and the only boxcab switcher built after Alco left the GE-IR consortium. *Richard Jay Solomon*

commercially successful diesel-electric locomotive. It is preserved at the Baltimore & Ohio Railroad Museum in Baltimore.

Among the most unusual products of Alco-GE-IR were experimental road diesels built on the request of New York Central. These resembled Central straight electrics of the period. Built in 1928, New York Central No. 1550 has often been cited as the first road diesel in the United States. It was a 151-ton boxcab with a 2-D-2 wheel arrangement, powered by a 750-horsepower IR diesel. Another experimental was a center-cab, tri-power locomotive, No. 1525, designed to draw power from the Central's under-running, direct current, third-rail, or onboard batteries. The batteries were charged by a 300-horsepower IR diesel. This arrangement was conceptually similar to modern hybrid automobiles and switching locomotives. After tests with No. 1525, New York Central made the unprecedented decision to order a substantial fleet of boxcab tri-power locomotives from General Electric. John Kirkland notes in *Dawn of the Diesel Age* that while these had Alco builder's numbers, they were actually constructed by GE. Most of the Central's tri-power locomotives worked in the New York terminal area, but some were assigned to Chicago, Detroit, and Boston. (Another locomotive, built to New York Central specs, was delivered to Rock Island for switching at LaSalle Street Station in Chicago.)

Related to these developments was another boxcab road diesel ordered by New York Central in 1926 from Auburn, New York–based engine manufacturer McIntosh & Seymour (M&S). As with the Alco-GE-IR units, Alco built the mechanical portions of this machine. It was completed in 1928 and tested as New York Central No. 1500. Viewed in isolation, these forays into road diesels may seem like an anomaly on Alco's part. In fact, Alco's engineers had been paying close attention to diesel developments abroad and were well aware of their role in technological developments.

In the late 1920s, Alco recognized the value of the diesel-switcher market while acknowledging inherent flaws in the GE-IR product, as well as its own low level of input in the arrangement. Alco left the GE-IR consortium in 1930 to pursue its own diesel-switcher designs. By 1929, Alco had acquired a majority share in McIntosh & Seymour in order to advance its diesel engine technology for practical locomotive applications. This occurred a few months before General Motors' acquisitions of the Winton Engine Company and railcar builder Electro-Motive. McIntosh & Seymour was an established builder of stationary and marine engines. By 1930, it was producing a dozen varieties of internal combustion engines. Within two years, M&S's Auburn engineering group had refined two six-cylinder inline diesel engines for Alco locomotive applications. Kirkland explains that M&S's model 6-L-19-S became Alco's model 330, rated at 300 horsepower, while the 6-L-25-S became Alco's 531 engine, rated at 600 horsepower. Using these engines, Alco began constructing its own commercial diesel-electric switchers.

The 531 engine was a 12.5x13-inch, six-cylinder, four-cycle design operating at 700 rpm. The essence of the 531 was modified in 1938 to become the 538 engine and was further modified in 1939 into the extremely successful 539 engine. This latter design remained in production until the early 1960s, long after Alco had developed more powerful diesel engines.

Opposite: The distinctive Blunt truck was named for its designer, Alco engineer James G. Blunt. The Blunt trucks were standard equipment on Alco's pre-1950 switchers that featured a 96-inch wheelbase. Today, operative diesel locomotives with Blunt trucks are rarer than steam locomotives, yet a few survive. *Brian Solomon*

EARLY PRODUCTION SWITCHERS

Prior to 1936, Alco built more than 30 diesel switchers for commercial purposes, making it the leader in this new market. While the boxcab design was standard during the Alco-GE-IR era (and Alco's first solo effort was a similar 300-horsepower boxcab sold to Jay Street Connecting Railroad in downtown Brooklyn, New York), most of Alco's early production models used the end-cab hood designs. This style was established by Westinghouse's visibility-cab switchers of the same period. Where the Westinghouse design used essentially a tapered notch in the locomotive body to give crews a better view, Alco used a narrow sheetmetal hood over the engine and other primary components that provided narrow walkways on either side of the hood and a full-width driving cab at one end. This gave the locomotive engineer a view fore and aft without having to change ends. For switching duties, this arrangement was superior to

ALCO EMBRACES THE TURBOCHARGER

Among the pioneers of supercharging was Swiss inventor Dr. Albert J. Büchi. He began experimenting in 1905, and over the next two decades blended internal combustion and turbine technology in the form of a turbine-powered engine supercharger. Büchi began licensing his invention in 1927. A supercharger boosts output by compressing air to richen its oxygen content for a given volume; when paired with the appropriate quantity of fuel, this increases the engine's power output. The Büchi supercharger turbine is powered by engine exhaust, which spins a shaft, that in turn spins a compressor turbine in the engine's air-intake path. To distinguish from other types of superchargers, which use some form of direct engine drive, Büchi's system is often described as a turbo-supercharger, or more simply as a turbocharger.

Seeking to increase the output of its diesels, Alco's engineers began work with the supercharger pioneer as early as 1932. Over the next few years, Büchi's engineers helped Alco adapt the Büchi turbocharger to the 531 diesel. The success of this joint effort resulted in Alco licensing the Swiss Büchi system for use on the 531 engine in 1937. This improved engine was designated 531T and rated at 900 horsepower output. It did not replace the 600-horsepower 531 engine, and the two engines were produced concurrently. August 1937's *Diesel Railway Traction* reported that in order to employ Büchi technology, Alco needed to make some nominal engineering changes to its engine, including adjustments with the compression ratio, changes to the shape of intake and exhaust manifolds, and changes to camshaft timing.

At idle, the Büchi turbocharger turbine rotates at 3,000 rpm; as the engine is notched up, exhaust gases leave under greater pressure, increasing the speed of the turbine; at maximum throttle, it is spinning at about 12,000 rpm. Depending on the speed of the engine, air is forced into the cylinders at between 2 and 4 psi. Alco's pioneering American application of the turbocharger for diesel-electric locomotives set an important precedent for future development and application. Today, turbochargers are standard on modern high-horsepower locomotives.

Built in 1939–1940, the Milwaukee Road's four 660-horsepower high-hood Alco switchers were typical of Alco's production in that period. Powered by the 538 diesel, these rode on Blunt trucks and exhibited Kuhler's styling improvements. No. 1600 was photographed shortly after delivery at Milwaukee on April 24, 1940. Boston & Maine, Erie, Green Bay & Western, Lackawanna, Louisville & Nashville, Maine Central, New Haven, Northern Pacific, Southern Pacific, and Wabash were among the railroads that ordered similar locomotives. *Ted Schneff collection, courtesy Jay Williams*

double-ended box cabs with separate cabs at each end of the locomotive. The hood arrangement conveniently mimicked the locomotive design of the typical steam locomotive, so crews who were used to looking down the length of the boiler would find a familiar view looking down the diesel's hood.

Beginning in 1931, Alco switchers used the distinctive cast-steel Blunt truck, named for its designer, James G. Blunt. This truck was intended to negotiate the poor track typical of industrial sidings, where switchers tended to work. In 1936, Alco began production of 600-horsepower and 900-horsepower switchers that conformed with recently established industry standards.

To improve the appearance of its switchers, Alco turned to Otto Kuhler, best known for his subsequent work on the Alco-built *Hiawatha* streamlined steam locomotives discussed in Chapter 2 and Alco's later road diesels. One of Kuhler's first assignments with Alco was the 1934 restyling of the 600-horsepower switcher. Although not a showcase design, Kuhler's refinement resulted in a distinctive-looking machine. He raised the top of the hood to match the roofline of the cab, recessed the headlights, and implemented a variety of minor aesthetic improvements.

In its early diesel production, Alco employed electrical gears from both major suppliers: General Electric and Westinghouse. This changed in 1940, when Alco entered an agreement with General Electric as its sole electrical supplier. By this time, GE and IR had ended production of boxcab diesels. For the next dozen years, Alco and GE engaged in a joint production and marketing arrangement in the sale of diesel-electric locomotives. Their diesels were sold as Alco-GE products. General Electric not only supplied electrical components but also was involved in other elements of engineering, including the styling of the postwar road diesels.

Boston & Albany No. 682 was an Alco 600-horsepower switcher built in April 1939 as part of an order for 11 locomotives. It was powered by an inline six-cylinder 531 engine. In later years, this type was known as an HH600. The inline six in Alco's high-hood switchers faced in the opposite direction from those in its S-unit switchers built from 1940 onward. *Alco builder's card, Robert A. Buck collection*

CLASSIFYING THE EARLY ALCO SWITCHERS

In its early years of diesel production, Alco did not use model designations to describe its offerings. Buyers knew its locomotives by their type and output, and internally by their specification numbers. To distinguish the early production switchers from the later S models, locomotive chroniclers have descriptively called these locomotives "high-hoods" and retroactively applied designations: HH600 and HH900 to the 600- and 900-horsepower locomotives built between 1931 and 1939; and HH660 and HH1000 to the 660- and 1,000-horsepower switchers constructed between 1939 and 1940, a change that reflected increased output offered by the 539/539T engines. In *The Diesel Builders, Vol. 2*, Kirkland notes emphatically that Alco never used these designations. Production totals published in Jerry Pinkepank's *Diesel Spotter's Guide* indicate that 183 high-hood switchers were constructed through 1940, when the type was discontinued.

S-MODEL SWITCHERS

Despite the widely publicized introduction of diesel-powered, articulated, streamlined trains built by General Motors' Electro-Motive Corporation (known as GM's Electro-Motive Division after 1940), throughout the 1930s the diesel switcher remained the most important and competitive element of the diesel-electric market. EMC had begun to produce diesel switchers in 1935 using the compact, high-output, Winton 201A engine. Baldwin also entered the market, building switchers starting in 1939.

One of the advantages of EMC's switcher design was a lower hood, made possible by the smaller size of the Winton (and later the 567) engine. This gave the locomotive engineer better visibility than Alco's high-hood designs. In 1940, Alco introduced two new switchers to accompany the new and more compact model 539 engines that permitted frame-mounting. This enabled the hood to be redesigned with a profile 2 feet, 3 inches lower, which improved visibility from the cab. Two windows were added, giving a view over the top of the hood. Like the high-hoods, the output of the two switchers differed because of engine type. The 660-horsepower model S-1 used the

In 1939–1940, Alco redesigned its diesel engine, creating the new model 539 to permit lower mounting, which enabled a reconfiguration of the hood for better visibility. The position of the engine was reversed, which put the radiators at the end of the hood instead of close to the cab. New switcher models were introduced in 1940. In February 1960, New York Central S-2 No. 8569 switches autoracks carrying new Studebakers at West Albany, New York. This photo foreshadowed an interesting and ironic corporate juxtaposition: Worthington, which bought Alco Products in 1965, merged with Studebaker in 1967 to form Studebaker-Worthington. Car production ended prior to the merger, and Alco's locomotive production ended in 1969. *Jim Shaughnessy*

normally aspirated six-cylinder 539 engine, while the 1,000-horsepower S-2 used the six-cylinder Büchi turbocharged 539T. Both rode on Blunt trucks.

The S-1/S-2 switchers were simple, functional, well-built machines and, as a result, they were among Alco's best-selling diesel designs. They had a handsome and well-balanced utilitarian design that was basic, but not unpleasant to look at. Both Alco types used welded frames, a relatively new technology at the time; some of Electro-Motive's and most of Baldwin's early switchers had used cast frames. Between coupler faces, the Alcos measured 45 feet, 5.75 inches long and featured cabs with elliptical-top roofs that were 14 feet, 6 inches tall at the apex. One variation of the S-1 that was ordered by the New Haven Railroad used a less-elegant low-clearance cab for work in tight clearances and electrified territory.

The S-1 and S-2 appear similar externally and employ the standard B-B wheel arrangement typical of American diesel switchers (all four axles powered). The most obvious distinguishing feature is the size of the radiator vents on the sides of the hood. With the redesign of the hood, the radiators had been moved toward the front of the locomotive. The size of the vents reflects engine

Maine Central S-1 No. 953, working as the Lewiston switcher, assembles a circus train at Lewiston, Maine, on July 21, 1974. On the right is a searchlight block signal. The signal arm on the left holds a blue light that indicates there is an unsignaled track between the signal and the track governed by the signal. Once common, such signals have become relatively unusual in New England.
George S. Pitarys

The Erie's significant purchases from Alco continued into the diesel era. On April 16, 1948, Erie S-1 switcher No. 312 rests along a set of FA/FB road diesels at the Meadville diesel shop. The 660-horsepower S-1 can be readily identified by its combination of narrow radiator and Blunt trucks.
J. William Vigrass

Southern Railway S-2 No. 2229 was about 25 years old at the time of this photograph at Columbia, South Carolina, on September 4, 1970. The ubiquitous Alco switcher was hardly worth a passing glance for the gathered crowd trackside, which was out to catch a glimpse of the Southern's No. 4501, the famous Baldwin Mikado that was leading a National Railway Historical Society excursion from Washington, D.C., to Charleston, South Carolina. Today, the S-2 is just a memory, but old No. 4501 survives. *George W. Kowanski*

capacity; the turbocharged S-2 required greater radiator capacity than the normally aspirated S-1. So, where the radiator on the S-2 measures about half the length of the Blunt truck, the radiator is less than half the length of the truck on the S-1. Based on published specifications, an as-built S-2 weighed 230,000 pounds. The S-1 was 30,000 pounds lighter.

General Electric's electrical equipment included a GT-552 main generator and GMG-139 auxiliary generator. Traction motors were the standard GE-731 models, nose-suspended in typical American practice. The S-1 had about 50,000 pounds continuous tractive effort, while its rating with the standard 75:16 gear ratio (the numbers reflect the teeth on the driving axle bull gear and traction motor pinion gear) at 6.1 miles per hour continuous speed was 29,200 pounds (based on an estimated 30-percent adhesion). Likewise, an S-2 with 75:16 gearing had starting a tractive effort of about 69,000 pounds and delivered 34,000 pounds continuous tractive effort at 8 miles per hour minimum continuous speed. Maximum safe speed was 60 miles per hour. The S-2 was by far the more common of the two types. Pinkepank states that 1,825 S-2s were sold in North America, compared with 724 S-1s.

In 1950, Alco introduced new models, including improved switcher types. The 660-horsepower S-3 replaced the S-1, and the 1,000-horsepower S-4 replaced the S-2. The basic equipment and layout of the locomotives remained the same, and horsepower ratings remained unchanged. Among

Manufacturers Railway Company No. 212, at St. Louis in November 1981, is a classic example of Alco's 1,000-horsepower model S-4 switcher. It was bought new from Alco in 1951 by the Anheuser-Busch–owned switching line. The large radiator distinguishes it from the 600-horsepower S-1/S-3, while use of the swing-equalizer, drop-bolster, AAR type-A trucks distinguishes it from the otherwise-similar model S-2 with the Blunt-type truck. The railroad's once all-Alco switcher fleet was augmented with Electro-Motive units in the mid-1970s, and the Alcos gradually retired. *Scott Muskopf*

This Livonia, Avon & Lakeville Alco was built in July 1941, making it one of the earlier S-2 switchers. During World War II, the War Production Board limited Alco's production, yet it was allowed to produce switchers and continued building the model S-2 through the war. Alco continued to build the 1,000-horsepower S-2 until June 1950, when the model was superseded by the S-4. *Brian Solomon*

the most significant differences was the switch from the Blunt truck to the more conventional drop-bolster AAR (Association of American Railroads) type A truck.

In their heyday, Alco switchers were assigned switching duties everywhere. They worked local freights, toiled on industrial sidings, meandered down branch lines, and worked in coach yards and in passenger terminals. They were part of the fabric of the railway for more than a generation and were well liked by engineers for their pulling ability. Yet, because they were so ordinary they were hardly noticed by diesel watchers until they had nearly vanished from Class 1 railroads. Although most have been scrapped, a few survive today working in obscure places, often on industrial sidings, such as those used by electricity-generating stations and grain elevators.

ROAD SWITCHERS

Not long after introducing S-unit switchers in 1940, at the request of Rock Island Lines, Alco expanded its switcher design into a road-switcher type that would be capable of performing both switching and road duties. Rock Island's resourceful chief operating officer, J. D. Farrington, hoped to reduce branch-line expenses by replacing steam locomotives with these versatile, multiple-application diesels. Later known by the model designation "RS-1," the road-switcher became one of Alco's most versatile locomotives, with production spanning 18 years.

New York, Susquehanna & Western was an early purchaser of Alco's RS-1 road-switchers. These were used in both freight and passenger service beginning in 1942. In January 1963, NYS&W No. 238 works a commuter train, 18 years after it was bought new from Alco in 1945. *Richard Jay Solomon*

Penn Central RS-1s work at the Goodman Street yard office in Rochester, New York, on June 24, 1972. The Penn Central inherited RS-1s from all three of its component railroads. PC No. 9908 was formerly New York Central's No. 8108, built in March 1948, while No. 9930 was a former Pennsylvania Railroad unit built in 1950. These old 539-powered road-switchers survived long enough to be included in Conrail. *R. R. Richardson, Doug Eisele collection*

Opposite, bottom: The Rock Island encouraged Alco to adapt its 1,000-horsepower S-2 switcher into a new type called a "road-switcher"—in other words, a multi-purpose diesel-electric. No. 747 was built in 1941; it rode on swing-equalizer, drop-bolster trucks made by General Steel Casting Corporation rather than the standard Blunt trucks used on the switchers. By 1942, the railway trade press had identified the virtues of the road-switcher, and by 1952, it was the dominant type of new locomotive in North America. The RS-1 model remained in production for nearly 20 years, despite Alco's introduction of more powerful road-switchers after World War II. *Alco builder's card, author collection*

The RS-1's multifaceted utility was a significant development, although mechanically it shared the basics established by Alco's 1,000-horsepower switcher. The RS-1 rode on a longer frame, was equipped with road trucks, and had a short hood on one end that could house a steam generator to provide steam heat for passenger cars. Like the S-unit switcher, the hood configuration gave crews good visibility for switching while allowing the locomotive to operate in either direction, yet its longer wheelbase (40 feet, 4 inches compared with 30 feet, 6 inches on the switchers), swing-equalizer, drop-bolster truck design; and gearing enabled it to operate at track speeds. The hood arrangement was also well suited for routine servicing at outlying locations. Like the S-2, the RS-1 was powered by the 1,000-horsepower, six-cylinder 539T engine and equivalent GE electrical components, and it was capable of up to 70 miles per hour (depending on the gear ratio). Although its longer wheelbase limited its use on tight industrial tracks, the RS-1 could perform most of the yard switching duties of the S-unit switchers. Where earlier diesel types were designed for specific tasks—switching, long-distance high-speed passenger trains, or heavy freight—the RS-1 was intended for a variety of assignments.

Above: An Ann Arbor RS-1 leads three cars on the eastward Cadillac Turn from Elberta across Michigan's Manistee River in August 1973. *Terry Norton*

The Milwaukee Road's two DL109 road passenger locomotives, Nos. 14A and 14B, were bought in 1941 for high-speed *Hiawatha* passenger services. Half the pair was displayed at the Chicago Railroad Fair in 1950. *C. Richard Neumiller*

Many authorities cite the RS-1 as the first true diesel-electric road-switcher. This type demonstrated great versatility inherent to diesel-electric locomotives. Nevertheless, while Alco recognized the universality of the new breed of locomotive it had created, it failed to take full advantage of this innovation. In the decade after the introduction of the RS-1, railroads and locomotive builders continued primarily to build and use specialized locomotive types. It wasn't until the early 1950s that the road-switcher became the dominant type of railway locomotive. By that time, the ability of one locomotive to do virtually all types of work had developed great appeal. Unfortunately for Alco, by the time the road-switcher matured, the manufacturer had lost substantial market share; by the 1950s and 1960s, the most popular road-switchers in America were EMDs.

By design, the RS-1 was ideal for branch line service. Greater reliability and fewer servicing requirements gave the locomotive twice the availability of typical branch line steam power. The diesel engine afforded additional savings because it required substantially less maintenance and had higher availability than steam. One diesel could effectively replace more than one steam

The Santa Fe's only DL109/DL110 pair poses for a publicity photo shortly after delivery in 1941. Nos. 50 and 50A were dressed in an adaptation of the Santa Fe's famous warbonnet paint scheme, designed by Electro-Motive's Leland A. Knickerbocker. These unusual locomotives were scrapped in the autumn of 1960. *Santa Fe publicity photo, W. A. Lucas collection, Railroad Museum of Pennsylvania PHMC*

locomotive. The RS-1's excellent fuel economy was another benefit. The first two were sold to Rock Island in 1941. The railroad assigned the locomotives to work between Burlington, Iowa, and Sioux Falls, South Dakota. Initially, four RS-1s were allocated to do the work of seven steam locomotives. However, by changing the servicing location to the more central point of Cedar Rapids, Rock Island found that it only required three RS-1s for freight work on this run. It reassigned the fourth locomotive to work the 180-mile round trip between St. Joseph, Missouri, and Topeka, Kansas. In the RS-1's early years, the railroad boasted it had 97 percent availability and found the road-switcher was suitable for moving trains up to 1,350 tons on grades up to 1 percent.

During World War II, the U.S. Army deemed the RS-1 especially well suited to military applications, and it ordered variations for work overseas. Many used three-axle, three-motor trucks, rather than the two-axle AAR trucks used on civilian locomotives. Alco also built an export model of the RS-1 that used A1A trucks to achieve lighter axle loadings. While some diesel writers have retroactively applied the RSD-1 and RSC-1 model designations to the C-C and A1A variations, Kirkland noted in *The Diesel Builders, Vol. 2* that Alco didn't make this distinction. Alco designated types E1640, E1641, and E1641A for the B-B locomotives; E1645, E1646, and E1647 for the C-Cs; and E1651 for the A1A-A1As. Through the army's adoption of Alco's road-switcher, adaptations of the basic type were introduced to the Soviet Union (Soviet RS-1s were near copies of U.S. Army locomotives). To this day, many Alco-derived road-switchers work in the former Soviet empire.

The RS-1 remained in domestic production until 1951 and in export production until 1960. A total of 623 RS-1s were built. The 1,000-horsepower 539T prime mover was used even after more modern engine designs were introduced. The RS-1 proved to be one of Alco's most enduring diesels, and today a few vintage RS-1s still operate on short lines.

PREWAR ROAD LOCOMOTIVE

Through the 1930s, railroad traffic was soft compared with the Roaring Twenties, and so the market for road locomotives was poor. Yet during these Depression doldrums, GM's Electro-Motive introduced the first successful diesel streamlined passenger trains. Within a few years, its diesel applications had evolved the streamlined trains' power car design into the standalone streamlined E-unit. The E-unit was capable of hauling conventional heavyweight passenger trains as well as light streamlined consists. The first E-units were sold to the Santa Fe, Baltimore & Ohio and Union Pacific between 1937 and 1938. The E-unit entered regular production in 1939, using Electro-Motive's new model 12-567 engine in place of the Winton 201A engine used in the early locomotives. Electro-Motive's E-unit set the design pattern for high-speed passenger diesels, a pattern that was later emulated by Alco and other builders. Alco followed GM's concept of a streamlined-carbody style powered by dual prime movers riding on pair of A1A trucks (center axle unpowered), with multiple-unit capability and cabless B-units.

Alco began work on its road diesel in 1938, and in 1940, it was ready for demonstration. The 2,000-horsepower, high-speed, streamlined-carbody locomotive was clearly a conceptual clone of the E-unit, but it was distinguished by Otto Kuhler's styling. Its futuristic slanted nose and three-piece windshield presented a visual contrast to the automotive styling characterizing GM's products. Its carbody construction consisted of 3/16-inch steel sheetmetal.

Rock Island bought the prototype, which was powered by twin 538T engines. Unlike the E-unit, Alco's road diesel was intended for dual service and was offered with a wide variety of gear ratios allowing for various top speeds, ranging from 80 to 120 miles per hour depending on intended application. A handful of similar locomotives followed. Most of Alco's production units carried specification numbers: DL109 for the cabs and DL110 for cabless boosters. (Some early locomotives appear to have been retroactively assigned different specifications, which results in some confusion. The prototype was often described as a DL103b, while the first two production locomotives are described as DL105s and the next two DL107s. Differences between these locomotives are minor, and Alco did not assign them model designations. Kirkland insists that these specification numbers were invented after the fact.)

The DL109 and DL110 carbodies measured 74 feet, 4 inches and 72 feet, 4 inches, respectively (slightly shorter than the prototype). They were 9 feet, 10.5 inches wide, and 13 feet, 6 inches tall (maximum height including auxiliary equipment was 14 feet, 4 inches). They were powered by Alco's new 539T engine and rated the same as 538T-powered prototypes, so each unit delivered 2,000 horsepower. Each locomotive had two GE-726 traction motors per truck.

There was only nominal interest in Alco's 2,000-horsepower road diesel compared with Electro-Motive's E-unit. This can be partly attributed to War Production Board restrictions that greatly limited road diesel allocation between 1942 and 1945 and assigned most road diesel production to Electro-Motive. However, the WPB permitted Alco to build a few DL109s because they were designated as a dual-service type. This was done to overcome strict restrictions that prohibited construction of passenger locomotives during the height of the war. The final DL109s were built in 1945, by which time Alco was advancing better designs that entered production the following year.

The New Haven Railroad had greatest enthusiasm for Alco's DL109, ultimately purchasing 60 of the type—the bulk of production. These were painted in an attractive dark green with gold striping—similar to the New Haven's electrics. As the New Haven's first road diesels, they were largely assigned to passenger work during the day and freight at night. This dual-service application dictated 80-mile-per-hour gearing. August 1942's *Diesel Railway Traction* reported the New Haven typically assigned each locomotive two round trips daily on the 157-mile Boston-to-New Haven run. Locomotives were serviced at Boston with only 40 to 75 minutes needed to turn them around between runs. At New Haven, diesels were exchanged for straight electrics for the trip to New York City. The New Haven had advanced signaling, so the DL109s were equipped with automatic train control.

New Haven DL109 No. 705 leads an extra train at Providence, Rhode Island, in the early 1950s. The New Haven's 60 DL109s represented the bulk of Alco's production. These worked passenger services on the 157-mile run from Boston's South Station to New Haven, where electrics took over for the rest of the journey to New York City. Because they were intended for dual service, they used 19:64 gearing and GE-726 traction motors for 80 miles-per-hour maximum speed.

This rare photograph shows the back of New Haven DL109 No. 743 backing onto its train at Providence, Rhode Island, in the early 1950s. The New Haven assigned DL109s singly and in pairs to its Shoreline passenger services. Observers who witnessed the locomotives working full-throttle at speed noted they had a distinctive turbocharged whistle that sounded quite different from other 539-powered engines. *Both Leo King, courtesy Center for Railroad Photography and Art*

Detail of the Alco logo on an S-type switcher. *Brian Solomon*

CHAPTER FOUR

244 DIESELS

Opposite: Erie Lackawanna inherited RS-3s from both of its predecessors. In June 1971, the roar of 12-244s announces the passing of a westward freight on the former Erie Railroad at Tuxedo, New York. On Friday nights, the EL would round up commuter service locomotives, such as these RS-3s, and assign them road freights working between Croxton Yard and Port Jervis, New York. This would allow locomotives to do double duty and be returned in time for the Monday-morning rush.
George W. Kowanski

World War II exerted tremendous influence on American railroad operations and engineering, shaping locomotive development and acquisition. The war produced the greatest traffic surge in American railroad history. On some routes, wartime traffic was more than five times greater than during the Depression years. As railroads sought to cope with traffic-saturated main lines, they developed a voracious demand for new locomotives. Yet priorities for war munitions took precedent over domestic requirements, and shortages of key materials required for locomotive construction resulted in government-mandated restrictions and limitations on domestic locomotive production. This resulted in a difficult situation for both railroads and locomotive manufacturers. The low ebb of traffic during the Depression had resulted in many railroads under-investing in locomotives, and the surge of war traffic found most lines pressed for motive power. Road diesels had just been introduced before the war and only represented a tiny portion of the motive power available. Most lines had to get by with aging steam locomotives, many more than 30 or 40 years old.

Many railroads sought to buy diesels, but War Production Board restrictions in effect from April 1942 limited orders while imposing tight controls on the implementation of new locomotive designs. The WPB also limited the types of locomotives each of the major builders was allowed to

Shop forces at Delaware & Hudson's Colonie Shops in New York lift a 16-244 engine from one of the former Santa Fe PAs. The 16-244 was plagued with reliability problems, which hurt PA sales and contributed to Alco's poor standing with some railroads. *Jim Shaughnessy*

manufacture in order to minimize difficulties with parts distribution. Despite requiring approval for specific locomotive orders and opposing design changes, the WPB did not specifically prohibit research and development.

Although Alco was a pioneer diesel builder in the 1930s, it had been technologically eclipsed by advances introduced by its competitor, General Motors' Electro-Motive Corporation. The reasons for Alco's failure to stay abreast of diesel technology have been analyzed by Albert J. Churella in *From Steam to Diesel*, Richard Steinbrenner in *The American Locomotive Company: A Centennial Remembrance*, and other comprehensive railroad-industry histories (see Sources). In the 1930s, Alco was suffering financially as a result of the lack of business. The company remained committed to steam technology and failed to recognize how quickly American railroads would embrace dieselization once practical, reliable road diesels were made available.

In 1940, Alco recognized that its heavy 539 engine was inadequate to compete with Electro-Motive's new 16-567 engine. Alco needed a modern, lightweight design to stay in the running. By this time, Alco was already several years behind in technological development. It reacted to Electro-Motive's lead and continued to refine diesel designs, but fell further behind while being hampered by inadequate resources and then by the effects of war demands on its business.

In the early 1940s, Alco's Auburn engineering department had worked to develop a lightweight, high-output engine that would rival Electro-Motive's 567, called the 241 engine. This state-of-the-art, four-cycle diesel with 9x10 1/2-inch cylinders was intended, in a 12-cylinder configuration, to develop 1,500 horsepower and, in a 16-cylinder configuration, 2,000 horsepower. It was a break from Alco's established 539 engine and was designed for a new line of road locomotives to compete with Electro-Motive's E-unit and FT diesels. During the crush of wartime production, when Alco's resources were focused on the construction of hundreds of steam locomotives for export, as well as 539 diesels and war munitions, 241 development was not a high priority, and so the design progressed slowly. By 1943, the success of Electro-Motive road diesels caused Alco to recognize that without a high-output engine, its diesel-electric business would falter, and it allocated more resources to engine development. However, internal fights at Alco and continued indecisiveness as to the role of the diesel-electric in a postwar economy contributed to misguided development efforts. The 241 project was transferred from Auburn to Schenectady, and some of the Auburn-based engineers who had led the effort were sidestepped in favor of a new engineering team. The Büchi turbocharging system was abandoned in favor of development of a GE-designed aircraft turbocharger.

Then in 1944–1945, the 241 project was bypassed in favor of another new engine design, designated 244, which Alco's top management hoped would be better suited to inexpensive mass production. Despite more than three years of research and development, Alco dropped the 241 before it entered regular production and focused on the 244 engine. The 244 was derived from elements of the 241 design, yet it featured several fundamental design differences. Where the 241 used a wet block, the 244 featured a dry block with a water jacket.

As World War II was coming to a close, WPB restrictions were eased and the market was again open for locomotive production. Electro-Motive had a clear advantage because it had developed road-locomotive designs before the war and benefited from more than three years of intensive road testing without facing competitive realities. By contrast, Alco was fumbling in the development stages. Alco faced tough prospects, and it needed to make its road locomotives available as soon as possible or face extinction in the diesel market. While some traditionalists within the company still clung to the prospect of maintaining its steam locomotive business, by 1945, this idea was clearly doomed. Management deemed the 241 engine inadequate for regular production, and although the 244 had not benefited from adequate testing, it was pushed into production in 1946. After-the-fact analysis of Alco's technology by Kirkland, Steinbrenner, and others found that because Alco failed to sufficiently test and refine the 244, costly design flaws plagued its early production. Yet the 244 was to power the bulk of Alco's postwar road-diesel production.

The success of EMD's 5,400-horsepower model FT freight diesel and 2,000-horsepower E-units set the pattern that Alco followed in its own postwar models. Prior to regular production, Alco released a curious experimental A-B-A road diesel in September 1945. This was an oddly styled, three-unit prototype (DL203-1 for the A-unit and DL203-2 for the B-unit) with Otto Kuhler styling that looked like a squashed version of the DL109. The A-units measured 51 feet, 6 inches, making them roughly 23 feet shorter than the DL109. These rode on an unusual variety of B trucks. Because the 244 engine wasn't ready, the prototype was powered with the experimental 12-241 engine rated

at 1,500 horsepower. The experimental locomotive has come to be known by its somber nickname, *Black Maria* (pronounced with a long *i*), which reflected its uniform black paint and a near-total lack of lettering. Its failure foreshadowed the path of Alco's entire locomotive business. It began tests on the Delaware & Hudson in September 1945, and later underwent more extensive tests on the New Haven and the Bangor & Aroostook, where it was operated both as an A-B-A set and as separate units. Testing concluded in November 1946, and the experimental was cut up in 1947. By the time the *Black Maria* tests began, the 244 engine had already gained favor at Alco, and neither the 241 engine nor the DL203 locomotive entered production.

In January 1946, months before tests with the *Black Maria* concluded, Alco released the first of its new FA/FB 1,500-horsepower road freight locomotives for testing on the Delaware & Hudson. These locomotives featured an entirely different styling treatment developed by Alco's partner, GE, and were powered by the 12-244 rather than the 12-241. The 12-244 entered regular production in mid-1946.

A NEW ENGINE

In 1946, Alco introduced three road-diesel varieties powered by the recently engineered 244 engine. Instead of the Büchi supercharger used on the 539 engine, the 244 was equipped with GE's RD1 turbocharger, derived from a wartime aircraft turbocharger design and adapted experimentally on the 241. The 12-244 produced 1,500 horsepower, while the 16-cylinder produced 2,000 horsepower—the parameters originally outlined by Alco's 241 design. In its original configuration, the 12-cylinder 244 engine idled at 350 rpm and worked at full throttle at 1,000 rpm to produce 1,500 horsepower. Alco's Schenectady plant produced the 244 engines, while the 539 engines used in switchers and the RS-1 remained the production domain of the former M&S plant at Auburn.

During World War II, Alco's locomotive line was dominated by steam production. Through the end of the war and despite advancement of diesel-electric design, steam power had remained the mainstay of the American locomotive fleet. Some Alco officials had envisioned a gradual transition in its product line as diesels became more dominant. However, after the war, only a few railroads, such as New York Central and Chesapeake & Ohio, remained interested in Alco's steam designs. Based on successful wartime experience with General Motors' road models, most railroads were planning to buy diesels. With the rush to fill orders, the pressure was on diesel builders to begin peacetime production.

ROAD FREIGHT MODEL FA/FB

The first of Alco's 244 diesels to leave Schenectady was the FA/FB road freight locomotive. Alco's primary road freight diesel was clearly patterned after EMD's FT. The FT carbody type was initially sold in four-unit sets in A-B or A-B-B-A configurations. Electro-Motive anticipated railroad labor concerns regarding the need for men to work each and every unit, so the early

Opposite: On October 3, 1945, Alco's unusual *Black Maria* experimentals (Nos. 1500a and 1500b) work a Delaware & Hudson passenger train at Plattsburg, New York. The only locomotives powered by Alco's ill-fated 241 diesel and riding on nonstandard trucks, these tested for several months on the D&H, New Haven, and Bangor & Aroostook. In addition to the two A-units, a cabless booster was also built. By 1946, Alco's FA/FB 1,500-horsepower road freight locomotive had entered production powered by the 12-244 engine. The *Black Maria* had no future and was sidelined. Photographs of the units in service are very rare. *Jay Williams collection*

The Erie Railroad aggressively dieselized its lines after World War II. It bought large numbers of Alco diesels, including most of the postwar types. Sets of three- and four-unit Alco FAs were commonly assigned to road freights, while PAs worked long-distance passenger trains. RS-2s and RS-3s worked local and suburban trains as well as freight. Erie FA-1 No. 734 rests between assignments at the Meadville, Pennsylvania, terminal. *C. Richard Neumiller*

A-B sets were intended to be semi-permanently drawbar-coupled. By the end of the war, this arrangement was deemed operationally restrictive, and EMD's postwar diesels featured ordinary couplers. With the introduction of the F3 model, EMD upped its per-unit horsepower from 1,350 to 1,500.

Alco-GE's road freight locomotive closely resembled Electro-Motive's in most respects. It was a 1,500-horsepower, streamlined, enclosed carbody type, built in both cab-equipped A-units and cabless B-units. It used a B-B wheel arrangement (*B* indicating two powered axles), which placed the full weight of the locomotive on the driving wheels. Internally, it followed the same essential mechanical and electric pattern used by virtually all American diesels built until that time: a high-output diesel turned a direct current generator to produce electricity for traction motors that were geared in a nose-suspended arrangement to driving axles. Alco employed a four-cycle diesel engine, and Electro-Motive a two-cycle.

Alco-GE wanted to ensure that its locomotives were easily distinguished from its competitors' products. Interestingly, it was GE, not Alco, that supplied the designer for their jointly marketed diesel-electrics. Railway historian John Gruber explains that Raymond E. Patten, an industrial designer specializing in appliances, helped shape the distinctive appearance of Alco and General Electric locomotives in the postwar years. Design patents applied for in 1946 and granted in 1949 confirm Patten's role in the PA/FA models. From 1940 to 1953, Alco and GE jointly marketed large road locomotives. Alco-GE distributed a six-page article in which Patten said their goal was, "A locomotive so distinctive and so powerful looking that it actually helps the railroads sell their services to passengers and shippers." From rough pencil sketches of the exterior, executives

Right: Alco's first production 1,500-horsepower freight locomotives were these FA-1s for the Gulf, Mobile & Ohio. Built in the last months of 1945, they were first tested on the Lehigh Valley in an Alco demonstrator livery. They display Patten's original styling with forward number boards on top of the cab, a flourish extending back from the cab to minimize water dripping over the cab door (as used on the PA-1s), and lower headlight grille placement (allowing for a more graceful nose profile). GM&O No. 731 was photographed on June 23, 1960, at Corinth, Mississippi.
C. Richard Neumiller

Above: Chicago, Rock Island & Pacific FA-1s lead a freight into the yard at Herrington, Kansas, on March 27, 1954. Rock Island was an important Alco customer in the builder's early diesel years. CRI&P DL103b No. 624, built in January 1940, was Alco's first 2,000-horsepower road diesel. A year later, the CRI&P encouraged Alco to design the pioneer road-switcher, and the first delivered was Rock Island No. 748. Alco's early relationship with Rock Island didn't last. Not long after this photograph, Rock Island sent these FAs to Alco's chief competitor, Electro-Motive, for rebuilding. Although the railroad acquired 10 Alco C-415s in 1966, the majority of its later locomotives were EMDs and GEs.
C. Richard Neumiller

The classic lines of Patten's FA carbody design ensured that no one confused the Alco-GE diesels with those of General Motors' Electro-Motive Division. Kewaunee, Green Bay & Western FA-1s lead a short freight through the streets of Winona, Minnesota, on May 30, 1954. The KGB&W was a subsidiary of the Green Bay & Western, a prosperous regional railroad that connected its namesake with Winona and operated one of the smallest and most obscure fleets of FA-1s. The KGB&W was finally absorbed into the parent company in 1969. *C. Richard Neumiller*

selected the basic design. The fluted headlight, "devised to obtain product identity and serve as a focal point," had to be changed to meet Interstate Commerce Commission regulations. Melbourne Brindle's painting for the August 1946 GE calendar and other early illustrations, for example, show the headlight grille before it was moved higher on the nose of the locomotive. After testing, the first road freight diesels were delivered to the Gulf, Mobile & Ohio in 1946. These prototype FAs reflected Patten's original styling with the lower headlight and grille placement. Later units had the higher grille placement that many observers have deemed more appealing.

In its early years, this type of locomotive was described in advertising and company literature as simply, the "Alco-G.E. 1,500 Diesel-Electric Road Freight Locomotive." As with other types, the model designations came later: the FA-1/FB-1 model indicated *F* for freight, *A* for A-unit, and *B* for the cabless booster. Internally, the types were known by builder specification numbers. The FA-1 and FA-2 model designations covered several minor design changes that were reflected by different specification numbers. In *The Diesel Builders, Vol. 2*, Kirkland details these changes. The first FA-1/FB-1 specification numbers were DL208/DL209. These units employed belt-driven fans and auxiliary equipment, in an arrangement comparable to Electro-Motive FT and F2 carbody types of the same period. Between January 1946 and April 1947, Alco's Schenectady plant built a total of 80 units to these specifications. They had welded steel underframes and weighed 230,000

New Haven No. 0416 leads an A-B-A set of Alco FA-1s on the Shoreline with a long road freight at Warwick, Rhode Island, in the mid-1950s. New Haven bought a substantial fleet of Alco diesels, operating them in all types of service. Its final Alcos were C-425s built in 1964. *Leo King, courtesy Center for Railroad Photography and Art*

pounds fully serviced. Between coupler faces, the FA-1 measured 51 feet, 6 inches, while the FB-1 was 50 feet, 2 inches. Both A- and B-units were 10 feet, 6 1/2 inches wide and 14 feet, 9 inches tall with driving wheels 40 inches in diameter. Three gear ratios were offered; the most common was 74:18 gearing designed for a 65-miles-per-hour maximum speed and 34,000 pounds continuous tractive effort at 13.5 miles per hour. (As described in Chapter 3, locomotive gearing is represented by two numbers. The first indicates the number of teeth on the bull [axle] gear; the second number indicates the teeth on the pinion gear connected to the motor. The gearing defined minimum continuous speed and maximum speed ranges.) These early units used GE's GT-564B traction generator and were equipped with either GE-726 or GE-731 traction motors. As previously described, these units used the 12-cylinder Alco 244 diesel engine.

In early 1947, Alco introduced a revised FA-1/FB-1 design, reflected by specification numbers DL208A and DL209A. Notably, this design dispensed with the belt-driven auxiliaries, replacing them with more reliable motor-driven equipment, a move consistent with changes to equivalent Electro-Motive models and already standard equipment on the 2,000-horsepower passenger diesel—model PA/PB (described in more detail later in this chapter). Electrical improvements

Alco FA-1 freight cabs were not equipped with steam generators and were rarely used in passenger service. The Tennessee Central was one of only a few railroads known to have regularly assigned FA-1s to passenger trains. On September 14, 1949, the TC's nearly new FA-1 No. 805 is at the east end of the line at Harriman, Tennessee. A young observer is more intrigued with the Railway Post Office than the new locomotive. TC train No. 1 was scheduled to depart Harriman at 12:01 p.m. for Nashville. *Howard R. Blackburn, Jay Williams collection*

boosted the continuous tractive effort rating to 42,550 pounds at 11 miles per hour. The traction generator was upgraded to GE's GT-564C model, and the durable GE-752 traction motor was introduced as standard equipment.

The GE-752 became a most successful traction motor and a fundamental component used by thousands of locomotives built from the 1940s. Not only was the GE-752 standard on Alco's road diesels, but in later years it was standard on most GE-built road locomotives. Although the motor has undergone a variety of improvements, it remains a common motor on many locomotives still in service today.

Nominal design changes resulted in FA-1/FB-1 specification numbers DL208B and DL209B. Then, in early 1950, Alco changed the specification to DL208C and DL209C to reflect a boost in the 12-cylinder 244 engine's output to 1,600 horsepower. (This corresponded to a similar power increase by Baldwin and Fairbanks-Morse, which also wished to show favorable specs when compared with Electro-Motive.)

Later in 1950, Alco made more significant changes to its road freight design, including the provision for a steam generator in both the A- and B-units. The changes covered by the DL212/DL213 specification delineated the new FA-2/FB-2 models. Previously, only the FB-1 units had space for a steam generator, but steam heat was required for passenger services in cold weather. Initially, Alco anticipated that demand for passenger locomotives would be satisfied by PA/PB and

West of Montreal, Canadian Pacific and Canadian National's respective double-track main lines run adjacent for many miles. Caught at speed from a parallel Canadian National passenger train, Canadian Pacific MLW-built FA-2 No. 4084 rolls with a freight past the station at Dorval in October 1964. *Richard Jay Solomon*

road-switcher types. By 1950, changes in the passenger train market encouraged Alco to make the FA/FB type more versatile. When equipped with steam generators, passenger-service units were designated FPA-2/FPB-2. Kirkland notes that among the changes to the FA-2 was an increase to its main generator rating that better matched the 1,600-horsepower 244 engine. Despite this change, railroads rarely assigned FAs to passenger service in the United States, although these and later models built by MLW were widely used in Canada for passenger service. (Incidentally, MLW-built FPA-2/FPB-2 units carried different specification numbers than those built by Alco Schenectady.) Kirkland adds that in 1954, the FA-2/FB-2 specifications were changed to DL212A/DL213A to reflect use of the improved 244G engine.

ROAD PASSENGER DIESEL

Alco-GE's postwar passenger offering effectively supplanted its DL109/DL110 types. In the summer of 1946, Alco debuted its 2,000-horsepower passenger locomotive, later known as the Alco PA (*P* for passenger, *A* for A-unit). Its carbody styling was the work of GE's Patten and shared essential design features with the FA/FB freight diesels (as discussed previously in this chapter).

Many observers have deemed Alco's PA the finest-looking passenger locomotive of all time. While similar to the FA models, the PA's longer frame accentuated Patten's industrial design. The PA's 6-foot-long nose section and three-axle A1A trucks (the center axle was unpowered for weight distribution) gave the locomotive a rare elegance and sense of power that has yet to be equaled in American locomotive design.

Alco specifications indicate the PA measured 65 feet, 8 inches long over the couplers, while the PB was slightly shorter. Alco-GE described these locomotives by their specification numbers and later assigned the PA designation, further delineated by PA-1 and PA-2 models. Initially, the type was powered by a 16-cylinder 244 diesel using GE's RD2 turbocharger, which produced 2,000 horsepower. According to Kirkland's *The Diesel Builders, Vol. 2*, the early PA/PB used GE-746A2 traction motors and a GT-566C1 traction generator. General Electric specified the 10-pole generator for the 2,000-horsepower locomotive.

Alco's passenger diesels are seen running in an A-B-A set, as Ray Patten intended them. Santa Fe PA/PB-1s lead the *California Limited* at Topeka, Kansas, on March 28, 1954. As per Alco's specifications, each unit had a 1,200-gallon fuel tank and carried 230 gallons of lubricating oil. The Santa Fe's PAs appeared in Alco advertising, which boasted that, "exceptionally low fuel and lubricating oil consumption rates and reduced maintenance permit low-cost, economical operation."
C. Richard Neumiller

Factory-fresh Nickel Plate Road PA-1s catch the evening glint working an eastward passenger train at Rocky River, Ohio, in 1948. To provide steam heat, the PA was equipped with a Vapor-Clarkson oil-fired steam generator. This was located at the rear of the locomotive and was designed to deliver 3,000 pounds of steam an hour. Diesels continued to supply steam well into the Amtrak era. By contrast, modern locomotives supply electric power for heat. *J. William Vigrass*

During the course of PA production, which ran from 1946 to 1953, Alco-GE introduced a variety of design improvements, including a change to GE-752 traction motors as standard equipment. With the PA-2, which replaced the original model type in 1950, horsepower was increased by 250 horsepower per unit, giving these later units a 2,250-horsepower rating. Alco built 297 PA/PB units for 16 different American railways. Although the model was demonstrated to Canadian Pacific and Canadian National, the Canadian lines did not order it.

Alco offered the type with four gear ratios. With 64:19 gearing, the PA was rated for 80-mile-per-hour service and 35,000 pounds continuous tractive effort at 17 miles per hour; 62:21 gearing offered a top speed of 90 miles per hour and 30,500 pounds continuous tractive effort at 20 miles per hour; 60:23 gearing brought 100 miles per hour and 27,000 pounds continuous tractive effort at 23 miles per hour; and 58:25 gearing gave 117 miles per hour and 24,000 pounds continuous tractive effort at 26 miles per hour.

After 1947, there were few applications for high-speed gearing, because the Interstate Commerce Commission introduced restrictive regulations regarding maximum train speeds. Railroads without advanced signaling systems, such as automatic train stop (ATS) or cab signals, were required to limit passenger train top speeds to 80 miles per hour. Only a few railroads, such as the Santa Fe, had equipped their lines for higher speeds. Using a basic ATS system, the Santa Fe continued to operate passenger trains at 90 miles per hour. Many other railroads that had

Alco's 75,000th locomotive, the first PA-1, No. 51, along with PB-1 51A, tested on the Lehigh Valley in 1946 before being painted for the Santa Fe. Dressed in a minimalist Alco-GE demonstrator scheme, Nos. 51 and 51A are testing on a westward Lehigh Valley passenger train at East Mauch Chunk, Pennsylvania.
W. A. Lucas collection, Railroad Museum of Pennsylvania PHMC

Above: After the Lehigh Valley tested Alco's first PA/PB set in 1948, it acquired a fleet of 14 PA-1s for long-distance passenger service on its routes between New York's Penn Station and Buffalo. These were dressed in a classy adaptation of its Cornell red livery.
W. A. Lucas collection, Railroad Museum of Pennsylvania PHMC

Right: Santa Fe No. 51 was the first Alco PA, a locomotive symbolically assigned Alco build number 75,000. After tests on the Lehigh Valley, it was painted in the famous warbonnet design and delivered to the Santa Fe for passenger service.
Santa Fe photo by Jacob Lofman, W. A. Lucas collection, Railroad Museum of Pennsylvania PHMC

operated faster services without advanced signaling couldn't justify the investment and instead slowed trains down.

The first PA was advertised as Alco's 75,000th locomotive, a total nimbly adjusted for maximum effect that in theory included production of Alco's various predecessors. This machine was given construction number 75,000. Initially, this unit was part of an A-B set that tested on Lehigh Valley. Later in 1946, a second A-unit was added and sold to the Santa Fe, becoming its Nos. 51, 51A, and 51B. Dressed in the Santa Fe's famous warbonnet livery, No. 51 and company were proudly displayed in Alco-GE's period advertising. It's ironic that the pioneer construction of Alco-GE's premier passenger locomotive—specially designed to be easily distinguished from Electro-Motive products—was dressed in that distinctive blend of red, yellow, black, and silver, a scheme devised by Electro-Motive artist Leland A. Knickerbocker for the Santa Fe. As hard as it might try, Alco couldn't seem to escape Electro-Motive's dominance of the locomotive business.

A 1947 Alco-GE ad featuring the Santa Fe's resplendent PA also echoed the tone set by similar Electro-Motive ads. The ad strained to differentiate superior qualities of Alco's 2,000-horsepower passenger locomotive, stating, "This mighty passenger locomotive is the answer to your demand for motive power that packs real earning power. Because its turbo-supercharged 16-cylinder Alco engine develops extremely high horsepower per pound of weight you can haul more pay load, roll up more passenger miles for every locomotive mile."

Ad copy subtly points out differences in the Alco product to potential locomotive buyers: "Its modern lines and high speeds will improve the merchandising of your passenger service. Three-axle trucks and low-axle loading reduce locomotive and track stresses. Exceptionally low fuel and lubricating oil consumption rates and reduced maintenance permit low-cost, economical operation."

Delaware & Hudson is probably the best-remembered operator of Alco PA diesels, yet it didn't buy them from Alco, but rather secondhand from the Santa Fe in 1967. D&H retained the basic elements of the Santa Fe's warbonnet paint scheme, substituting blue for red. In October 1968, one of D&H's classy PAs leads a passenger train not far from Schenectady, New York. By the time this slide was processed, Alco had ceased production. *Richard Jay Solomon*

It was no secret to locomotive buyers that Alco's primary competition for the PA was Electro-Motive's well-established E-unit. By the time the PA was marketed, the E-unit's essential design was nearly a decade old, although the latest model, the E7, was introduced in February 1945. While Alco's PA/PB units used a single 2,000-horsepower diesel, the E7 was powered by a pair of 12-cylinder 567 diesels rated at 1,000 horsepower each. The E7a was more than 6 feet longer than the PA. Alco's ads claimed that Electro-Motive's two-stroke 567 engine with a Roots blower was less efficient than the 16-244 engine.

In 1950, Alco increased the rating of the 16-244 engine to 2,250 horsepower with a nominal redesign. This was equivalent to improvements on the 12-244 engine introduced at the same time. The new PA-2/PB-2 model (specification DL104C/DL105C) produced equivalent horsepower to Electro-Motive's new model E8, introduced concurrently. To show off the improved diesel, Alco-GE built a demonstration set to power a GE promotional train.

Alco's troublesome 244 engine had been cited for lower PA/PB reliability compared with Electro-Motive's E-unit. This contributed to lower sales and, for most operators, shorter service lives. While Alco addressed some of the 244's problems in its 1950 redesign, the engine's reputation for low reliability remains part of the Alco legacy. The 16-244 had a worse reputation for failure than the 12-cylinder model.

All of the PA/PBs were out of service by about 1970, except for the Delaware & Hudson's four secondhand PAs from the Santa Fe. (D&H contracted Morrison-Knudsen to rebuild them with new 251 engines in 1975 and operated them on American rails until 1978, when they were sold to Ferrocarriles Nacionales de Mexico.) By comparison, the E-unit was sold to many more railroads and totaled more than 1,200 units. Many E-units remained in service through the 1980s, with a few of the type rebuilt for continued daily service into the 1990s.

Left: Delaware & Hudson's former Santa Fe PAs were sold in the late 1970s to Ferrocarriles Nacionales de Mexico, where they operated for many years. Doyle McCormack repatriated two of the units, one of which was severely damaged in a wreck. He has restored one of the locomotives and painted it for the Nickel Plate Road, one of 16 railroads in the United States to buy the model new from Alco. Originally built in 1948 as Santa Fe No. 62L, it became D&H No. 18 in 1967 before moving to Mexico in 1978. It is seen in the roundhouse at Portland, Oregon, on September 17, 2004. *Tom Kline*

Above: Delaware & Hudson Alco PA No. 17 leads Amtrak's southward *Laurentian* across the Mohawk River bridge at Cohoes, New York, on November 14, 1976. *Jim Shaughnessy*

Some railroads favored the PA type over the more common E-unit. Southern Pacific, with its rugged, heavily graded lines, was no minor player in the market for passenger diesels—SP had been the third largest conveyor of railroad passengers during the war and was by far the most significant passenger carrier in the West. Although it bought 17 E7s, initially operating them in A-B-B sets, it preferred to assign PA/PBs for its long-distance services in graded territory. On its mountain lines, the PAs offered distinct advantages equipped with dynamic brakes and rugged GE traction motors. Ultimately, SP was the largest customer for the PA/PB models.

POSTWAR ROAD-SWITCHERS

The last of the 244 diesel types introduced in 1946 soon proved to be Alco's most successful and influential diesel type. The 1,500-horsepower road-switcher was an advancement of the RS-1 and was designated as Alco-GE's "1500-Hp Diesel-Electric Combination Switching Locomotive." It used the same 12-cylinder 244 diesel and electrical equipment as the FA/FB models, and the first of these models was known as model RS-2 (specification number E1661).

Michigan's Detroit & Mackinac Railway bought the first RS-2s in November 1946. By 1948, it had acquired six RS-2s, and these worked for the railroad for more than 30 years. Originally rated at 1,500 horsepower, in the 1950s, Alco rebuilt and upgraded the D&M's RS-2s to 1,600 horsepower. D&M No. 466 was the second RS-2 finished by Alco, and on June 22, 1978, it loads cars onto railroad steam ferry *Chief Wawatum* at Mackinac City, destined for St. Ignace. *Terry Norton*

Uncertain of the road-switcher market, Alco offered a variation of the E1661 specification equipped with six-axle, four-motor trucks, later categorized as model RSC-2. Its A1A trucks reduced axle loading and also lowered tractive effort (because locomotive weight was divided over six axles instead of four), and so had limited applications compared with the B-B types. Union Pacific, which operated both variations, rated the RSC-2's continuous tractive effort at just under 40,000 pounds and its RS-2's at 62,500 pounds (gear ratios not indicated). Just 70 RSC-2s were sold to railroads in the United States. Although it was constructed in relatively small numbers, the RSC-2's production actually preceded production of the far more common four-axle RS-2 model.

As with the FA/FB models, Alco implemented improvements to its road-switchers, both to correct design imperfections and increase pulling power. As in the case of the road freight models, in 1947 Alco's RS-2 benefited from improvements to the traction system. From then on, the RS-2s were built with the GE-752 traction motor as standard equipment. Toward the end of RS-2 production in early 1950, output was boosted from 1,500 to 1,600 horsepower. Then, after April 1950, the name of the four-axle road-switcher model was changed from RS-2 to RS-3.

Milwaukee Road RSC-2 No. 594 leads a one-car freight across the bridge at Cannon Falls, Minnesota, in August 1972. The Milwaukee Road bought the RSC-2 for use on lines with light axle loads. *Terry Norton*

Lehigh & Hudson River RS-3 No. 1 leads Erie Railroad passenger cars on an excursion in June 1960. Built in 1950, this locomotive served the L&HR for 21 years. The L&HR was a bridge line that forwarded traffic from eastern Pennsylvania to the Maybrook, New York, gateway. *Richard Jay Solomon*

Because Alco-GE made incremental changes to the road-switcher line, there are few substantial differences that clearly differentiate between the RS-2 and RS-3 models, although there are some minor external differences; the location of a battery box beyond the cab on a short hood can distinguish the RS-3. Most RS-2s were rated at 1,500 horsepower, and all the RS-3s were 1,600 horsepower. Yet as noted with the FA/FB models, the horsepower increase does not offer a clear delineation for model change, nor did such a nominal power increase make for a substantial difference in locomotive performance. Confusing matters further, many 1,500-horsepower RS-2s were rebuilt and upgraded to 1,600 horsepower by Alco.

RS-2 and RS-3 road-switchers were versatile machines designed to work either singly or in multiple in freight, passenger, and switching service. They featured a semi-streamlined hood-unit configuration that was one of the most attractive road-switcher designs. Not only were they the

Originally Pennsylvania Railroad No. 8445, this was the railroad's sole RS-3 equipped with both dynamic brakes and a steam generator. The Penn Central later traded it to the Lehigh Valley, which renumbered it No. 211 (filling the spot in the LV's roster previously occupied by an RS-2). The unusual locomotive survived into the Conrail era and was rebuilt with a 12-567 engine as an RS-3m by Altoona shops. In the mid-1980s, it was bought by a private party and later donated to the Rochester Chapter National Railway Historical Society. In March 1975, it was photographed at Sayre, Pennsylvania. In 1990, it was repainted in Lehigh Valley paint and is maintained in operable condition at the museum at Industry, New York. *Doug Eisele*

most numerous Alco road locomotives from the mid-1940s until the early 1970s, Alco road-switchers were also among the most common locomotives in the United States, although more so in the East and Midwest. Louis A. Marre's *Diesel Locomotives: The First 50 Years* indicates that 366 RS-2s and 1,265 RS-3s were sold to lines in the United States. Alco's road-switchers too often went unnoticed at a time when many observers were focused on documenting the end of the steam era, and they were ultimately not as common as Electro-Motive's General Purpose models, GP7/GP9 (developed as General Motors' answer to Alco's successful road-switcher).

Many lines assigned Alco road-switchers to heavy freight work, typically working in multiple either with like models, Alco's FA/FB cabs, or, in later years, with other builders' models. Some railroads favored RS-2/RS-3s for suburban passenger operations because they accelerated quickly and could maintain schedules better than other types. The Boston & Maine, Central Railroad of New Jersey, Erie Railroad, Long Island Rail Road, New York Central, New Haven, Pennsylvania, Reading, and Rock Island all employed suburban service RS-2/RS-3 fleets. On some lines, Alco RS-2/RS-3s were routinely assigned to medium- and long-distance passenger services. For example, New York Central commonly used them on its less prestigious long-distance passenger trains, while the Delaware & Hudson assigned them to its *Laurentian* and *Adirondack*.

In December 1996, a few months before the merger between the Seaboard Air Line and the Atlantic Coast Line, SAL RS-3 No. 1633 leads a short freight at Tavaries, Florida, that originated at Wildwood. Running on the old Tavaries & Gulf, this freight served the citrus groves and processing plants in the region. *Terry Norton*

A pair of San Manuel Arizona Railroad Company RS-3s and a GP38 lead a train across a wooden trestle at Mammoth, Arizona, on December 13, 1986. SMARRC connected a copper smelter with an interchange with Southern Pacific near Hayden. The railroad's paint schemes were inspired by colors associated with copper. *John Leopard*

Canada's Pacific Great Eastern RSC-3 No. 562 leads converted troop sleepers. Notice the steam locomotive–style pilot. PGE's eight RSC-3s were later rebuilt with two-axle B trucks. PGE was renamed the British Columbia Railway in 1972 (later BC Rail) and was a large user of Alco and MLW locomotives. *Jay Williams collection*

SIX-MOTOR ROAD-SWITCHERS

Alco pioneered the six-motor concept during World War II, when it built six-motor RS-1s for the U.S. Army. Flaws with the six-axle truck design prevented easy access to the center traction motor, which discouraged Alco from selling six-motor RS-1s for domestic use.

Baldwin began selling six-motors in the late 1940s, yet the market for such locomotives was relatively small. A year ahead of Electro-Motive, Alco entered the domestic six-motor market in 1951 with its 1,600-horsepower model RSD-4. This was essentially an expanded version of the RS-3 with a larger generator, necessary to power six motors, and tri-mount trucks, which used a three-point suspension system for the three powered axles per truck. This design provided a smoother ride and greater stability at speeds up to 60 miles per hour as well as uniform weight distribution to all axles. The RSD-4 weighed 360,000 pounds, with 60,000 pounds on each axle. Unlike the four-motor RSC models that rode on three-axle trucks strictly to keep axle weight down, the RSD-4 benefited from its weight on driving wheels. Equipped with the 74:18 gear ratio, the RSD-4 was rated at 78,750 pounds continuous tractive effort at 5.5 miles per hour, compared with the RSC-3's 52,500 pounds at 8.5 miles per hour. A variation of the RSD-4, sometimes designated RSX-4, was built for the army. It featured a more utilitarian hood design for lower clearance. Kirkland highlights an interesting feature of this type in that it could be readily re-gauged for application to lines overseas. These types have been variously used by domestic railroads. For example, in the early 1950s, the New Haven Railroad assigned RSX-4s to freight service on lines in Rhode Island and Massachusetts.

In 1952, Alco upgraded its six-motor offering with the RSD-5, reflecting nominal specification changes but featuring the same basic characteristics of the RSD-4. Alco built a total of 240 RSD-4/RSD-5s between 1951 and 1956, of which 203 were for domestic use. Interestingly, this represented a large portion of the domestic six-motor diesel locomotive market at that time, yet these were bought for specialized heavy-freight applications and were never a common sight. Subsequently, American railroads had a growing interest in six-motor types. During the next few decades, six-motor road diesels evolved from an unusual special-service type to the preferred wheel arrangement for new road-service locomotives. While Alco offered a number of six-motor types, it failed to stay abreast of this market. Its later six-motor types remained a minority in the North American market.

One of four Canadian National Railways RSC-24s works east of Quebec City on a lightly built line near Ste. Anne de Beaupre. These unusual MLW locomotives were built in 1959 with A1A trucks and used recycled 244 engines taken out of FA/FB locomotives.
Jim Shaughnessy

MARKET POSITION

After the war, Alco-GE consistently held the number-two diesel market position, while Electro-Motive remained the clear industry leader—not just in sales, but in technological refinement. Albert J. Churella, in his book, *From Steam to Diesel*, explains that Alco-GE commanded roughly 40 percent of the diesel-electric market in 1946, but only 15 percent of the market in 1953. He presents a number of reasons for Alco's dramatic loss of business. Continued steam-era business practices were ineffective against Electro-Motive's philosophy of mass production derived from General Motors' automobile-building practices. Other problems were related to Alco's labor force. Traditionally, its employees had been better compensated than Electro-Motive's, which increased its production costs. Furthermore, after the war, Alco production was disrupted by strikes that interrupted production and delayed locomotive deliveries. These distractions interfered with production during the most intensive period of dieselization, further cutting into the builder's potential market share. Undeniable problems with locomotive reliability damaged the builder's reputation and contributed to its inability to secure large repeat orders in later years.

Despite this reputation, it would be an error to simply declare that Alco-GE products were bad locomotives. In fact, they offered a variety of favorable performance characteristics. These locomotives tended to provide higher horsepower and greater tractive effort than Electro-Motive's comparable products, and they were generally better regarded than diesels built by either Baldwin or Fairbanks-Morse. Yet many railroads found that Alco diesels required greater levels of maintenance than Electro-Motive's diesels. Specifically, a number of flaws were attributed to the early 244 engine design. Several authors have cited difficulties with the GE turbocharger. Others, including Kirkland, have indicated that problems with the engine stemmed from it being rushed into production without a sufficient period of testing. Had Alco spent more time testing the engine, its design flaws would have been revealed in time for Alco to work out solutions before the 244 entered regular production. As it happened, Alco phased out the 244 in the mid-1950s in favor of its more recently designed, adequately tested, and demonstrably more powerful and more reliable 251 diesel. By that time, Alco had built thousands of road locomotives equipped with the 244 engine. Time would reveal that these locomotives were not as durable as other types. Many of Alco's 244 diesels only outlasted the steam locomotives they replaced by a few years. On some railroads, they were in service for less than a decade when they were sidelined and either traded in for new locomotives or re-engined (often with Electro-Motive's highly successful 567). Some 244 Alcos had long service lives. On railroads that favored Alco diesels, such as the Delaware & Hudson, 244 diesels worked for more than three decades. Even today, a few short lines have continued to operate 244 diesels in regular service, but these are the exception rather than the rule.

Vermont's Rutland Railroad made the switch to diesel in the early 1950s using a fleet of six RS-1s, nine RS-3s, and a General Electric 70-ton switcher. In June 1960, its RS-3 fleet was laid up at the Rutland shop during a strike. Declining traffic and labor difficulties ultimately shut the railroad down, although portions were later reactivated by the Vermont Railway and Green Mountain Railroad. *Jim Shaughnessy*

Toledo, Peoria & Western C-424 No. 800 was bought new from Alco in 1964 and sold in the early 1980s to New Jersey's Morristown & Erie.
Brian Solomon

CHAPTER FIVE

251 DIESELS

Opposite: The Lehigh Valley was a loyal Alco customer right to the end. Century 628 No. 635 is resplendent in Cornell red at the LV's Sayre, Pennsylvania, shops on April 8, 1973. The LV's C-628s were delivered in an attractive white and black livery accentuated by a bright red Lehigh Valley flag on the sides.
Doug Eisele

In 1950, Alco set out to design a new engine that would overcome design flaws in the 244, consolidate its engine types, and make provision for substantially greater output. At that time, Alco was producing two variations of the inline 6-cylinder 539, as well as both 12-cylinder and 16-cylinder 244 diesels for its standard diesel locomotives. By comparison, Electro-Motive had essentially one engine design that varied output by the number of power assemblies. Electro-Motive's strategy simplified maintenance and parts supply.

Alco's engine development coincided with other changes in its locomotive production. In 1953, the Alco-GE partnership was dissolved, although the two companies continued to work together on some projects and GE remained Alco's electrical supplier. Significantly, Alco's locomotives were no longer jointly marketed with GE, which began development of its own heavy diesel-electric line, at first targeting the international market. In 1954, Alco introduced a new road-switcher body style on its DL600/DL600A (model RSD-7) that was powered with a 16-cylinder 244 engine rated at 2,250 horsepower. The boxier hood style was a substantial departure from the GE-designed locomotive styles introduced in the 1940s. The taller hood allowed Alco to offer both dynamic brakes and a steam generator as standard features. It had built a few RS-3s with both features for Pennsylvania Railroad and the Western Maryland, and

these locomotives featured unusually high short hoods as a result. (This incongruous-sounding description is a result of the layout of road-switcher type hood units whereby the two hoods are distinguished as "long" and "short" by length, and "high" and "low" by height.)

Alco's new engine entered development in 1951, retaining the essential dimensions of the 244 design: 9x10 1/2 bore and stroke. It was designated the 251 (the 2 in these designations infers the 9x10 1/2 dimensions). Alco drew on its experiences with the 244, 241, and 539 models; the new engine incorporated features of all three in what was to become its most successful and enduring design by far.

Many improvements introduced with the 251 were aimed at solving the high crankshaft-failure rate of the 244. Several changes were made to main crankshaft bearing design and placement. Significantly, main bearing seating was improved by dispensing with the tongue-and-groove alignment system used by the 244, instead adopting serrated edges between bearing caps and saddles that had been used by the 241. When the bearing caps were tightened down, the fixed serrated edges ensured a closer alignment. Main bearings were also larger, which nominally increased the length of the engine block. In addition, a more robust crankshaft was adopted.

Inadequate engine lubrication was another potential cause of bearing failure. Where the 244 had used internal fuel lines to the injectors, which risked contaminating or diluting the lubricating oil, the 251 engine returned to the 241's external fuel lines.

Another significant design change was dispensing with the 244's so-called "dry-block" design and returning to the 241's "wet block," where cylinder liners were located inside the block. In the early 1950s, Alco moved away from GE's RD-series turbochargers and re-adopted and refined the Büchi-derived turbocharger to its own design. While the GE turbocharger was air-cooled, the Büchi system was water-cooled. Alco also introduced an aftercooler, lowering the temperature of intake gases, thus allowing the turbocharger to increase the density of the intake charge supplied to the engine. Other changes included a general strengthening of the engine block, which continued to use fabricated cast-steel subassemblies. Alco's 244 diesels were famous for producing vast quantities of smoke as a result of poor combustion. The February 1956 issue of *Railway Age* noted that Alco adjusted governor timing to improve smoke emissions, explaining: "[The 251] governor provides timed rate of fuel advance that offers throttle-cushioned duty on the engine," and thus cleaner exhaust. The engine worked at a maximum speed of 1,000 rpm.

The improved design not only increased reliability, but made maintenance much easier. As Genesee Valley Transportation's Senior Road Foreman Matt Wronski has explained to this author, "The 251 is a charm to work on. It was a big improvement on the 539 and 244 engines. With the 251, Alco made it much easier to get at major parts. On the 244, Alco was still in 'steam mode,' and you needed to take off a lot of piping just to get at basic systems. By comparison, changing a water pump or turbocharger on a 251 is relatively easy. Everything is out in the open."

Alco began design with a basic engine configuration, the inline six-cylinder, which was intended to supplant the 539 engines for Alco's switcher and light road-switcher models. As this engine was

MLW IN THE DIESEL ERA

In the steam era, Montreal Locomotive Works was essentially Alco's Canadian subsidiary. Significant changes in this relationship coincided with the transition from steam to diesel production. In 1946, Alco divested three-fourths of its ownership in MLW, which Churella explains was used to fund diesel-related improvements to its Schenectady works. Canadian lines were slower to dieselize then their American ~~counterparts~~. While American firms pioneered commercial ~~diesel production, Ca~~nada effectively imported it, ~~and those selling to~~ the Canadian market were required ~~to produce locomotives the~~re. Initially, Alco built diesel ~~components for M~~LW to assemble. In *The Diesel Builders,* ~~Kirkland exp~~lains that the transition of manufacturing ~~spann~~ed the critical steam-to-diesel transition ~~years, from~~ 1948 to 1961. In the 1960s, MLW was entirely responsible for diesel manufacturing, although Alco still provided the majority of engineering. In addition to models built by Alco, MLW built a number of model variations and distinctive types unique to the Canadian market. In general, MLW fared better than Alco in the diesel market. Both large Canadian railways continued to place substantial orders for MLW diesels at a time when Alco was facing increased competition in the United States. When Alco exited the business in 1969, MLW inherited Alco's diesel engine and locomotive engineering legacy. Bombardier acquired MLW in 1975 and continued to engineer and build locomotives derived from Alco's designs into the 1980s.

On September 13, 1992, three C-424s and an M-630 lead CP Rail train No. 508 (Detroit, Michigan, to Montreal, Quebec) across the Trent River at Trenton, Ontario. The CP Rail was one of the significant operators of a large fleet of factory-bought Alco/MLW diesels. The six-motor M-630 was MLW's adaptation of Alco's C-630 model. *John Leopard*

Working northward from Montreal, CP M-630/M-636s and a former Norfolk Southern SD40-2 lead on the Trois Rivières train on January 12, 1993. *Brian Solomon*

This side-by-side comparison between Alco-built switchers at Stockton, California, in August 1975 displays external differences in hood style and radiator placement of its 539- and 251-powered S-model switchers. Central California Traction's 539-powered S-4 model on the right has side-mounted radiators (a common trait of the S-1 to S-4 models), while Southern Pacific's 251-powered S-6 on the left features the forward-facing radiator introduced on the S-5 model in 1954. *Brian Jennison*

refined and eased into production, Alco advanced to the more powerful V-12, and finally V-16, configurations. Kirkland points out in *The Diesel Builders, Vol. 2* that during development, Alco put the engine through its paces with ample amounts of testing to avoid the trap it fell into with the 244. By taking time to refine the engine and easing it into production cautiously, Alco finally achieved what General Motors had done a generation earlier: produce a reliable, compact, high-output diesel engine. The 251 proved to be a winner, and it soon replaced all of Alco's earlier designs for locomotives built for use in the United States. Montreal Locomotive Works continued to use the 244 and 539 engines for several years after those engines were discontinued in the United States. The 251 proved to be Alco's most enduring legacy to the new locomotive market. Into the mid-1980s, many years after Alco exited the locomotive business in the United States, the 251 was built in Canada for North American locomotive service. In addition, the engine has been built for a variety of stationary and marine applications, as well as for locomotive service around the world.

251 SWITCHERS

The first domestic application for the 251 was in 1954, when an inline six-cylinder model was adapted for Alco's new 800-horsepower model S-5 switcher (specification number DL421). In the December 1965 issue of *Trains*, Jerry Pinkepank described pre-production inline 251 diesels installed in 1953 on export locomotives built by GE for Cuba, and on some unusual narrow-gauge GE locomotives built for the White Pass & Yukon. Externally, the S-5 model used a revised radiator arrangement, noticeably different from the earlier S models. Instead of radiator intakes at the sides of the hood, a large intake vent faced forward on the hood and a vertically oriented fan drew air into the radiator, which then vented at the top of the hood. The S-5 was produced very briefly, and only seven were built, six of which went to the Boston & Maine. In 1955, Alco supplanted the S-5 when it introduced the 900-horsepower model S-6 (specification DL430).

Although 97 S-6 switchers were built for domestic applications, very few big railroads bought them. Southern Pacific represented the bulk of the production with 70 units. The Western Maryland had two, Northern Pacific bought one, and Belt Railway of Chicago bought one. Industrial lines and small railways accounted for the rest of the S-6s built for use in the United States. In addition, the S-6 was built for railroads in Mexico.

Domestically, Alco effectively replaced the S-6 in 1957 with model T-6 (specification DL440), which was powered by a 251B rated at 1,000 horsepower. Where *S* implied a switcher, *T* was used to designate a transfer locomotive. In most respects, there was little to distinguish the nature of these applications. The T-6 featured more modern styling and design, while it reverted to

Windsor & Handtsport's first day of operations finds three former CP Rail MLW RS-23s leading an empty gypsum train at Falmouth, Nova Scotia, on August 31, 1994. The W&H primarily hauled gypsum from mines east of Windsor to a transloading facility at Hantsport, where it was conveyed to ships for distribution around the world. The RS-23 was an adaptation of MLW's 1000-horsepower S-13 switcher that used trucks designed for road service. *John Leopard*

On April 20, 1972, Canadian National MLW-built S-13 No. 8623 works in Toronto. It is paired with a slug for greater tractive effort. *R. R. Richardson, Doug Eisele collection*

radiators situated at the sides of the hood. The front of the hood shared the style introduced on the RSD-7, with curved contours and a notched-nose front end. With this model, Alco finally supplanted its 539-powered switchers in the American market. Several models of 539-powered switchers continued to be built by MLW for use in Canada, including the 1,000-horsepower S-7 and S-12, and the 660-horsepower S-10 and S-11 (the S-11 and S-12 used the forward-facing radiator design, as did the Canadian-built 1,000-horsepower S-13 powered by a inline six-cylinder 251C engine). The T-6 remained in production until Alco exited the business. Its final domestic locomotives were a pair of T-6s built for the Newburg & South Shore. Alco's T-6 production totals were disappointing and numbered even fewer than its S-6. Norfolk & Western accounted for the bulk of production with 40 units. Pennsylvania Railroad bought six.

Low production figures on Alco's 251-powered switchers reflected changes in the market for low-horsepower locomotives, more so than indicating the failure of the design or manufacturer. Originally, switchers had been the largest market for diesels. In the 1940s and early 1950s, Alco had enjoyed robust switcher production. It built more than 2,600 S-1s to S-4s for the domestic market between 1940 and 1957. In addition, MLW produced large numbers of switchers in Canada. By comparison, Electro-Motive sold about 3,300 switchers in the 600-to-1,200-horsepower range between 1939 and 1954, while Baldwin built more than 1,875.

There are four important reasons for the rapid decline of switcher sales. The first was market saturation. Railroads had been sold on the cost savings afforded by the dieselization of switching operations. By the mid-1950s, American dieselization was nearing totality, and switching operations often had been first to be fully dieselized. Once dieselization was complete, railroads had little need for additional switchers. This explains why many of Alco's later switchers were not bought by the big American railroads, but by operators late to embrace dieselization, such as short lines and industrial lines, and also steam holdouts such as Norfolk & Western.

Second, switchers tended to be among the most rugged and reliable of all the diesels built. Alco's switchers were very well regarded for their pulling ability and availability. Electro-Motive's switchers were, and are, some of the most durable locomotives ever built. Even Baldwin, not

The Penn Central inherited Pennsylvania Railroad's fleet of T-6 switchers. Sunday, June 6, 1971, finds PC No. 9848 freshly painted, resting in the hazy morning sunlight of a very humid day at the Phillipsburg, New Jersey, yard. *Rich Zmijewski, courtesy Nick Zmijewski*

Alco's T-6 was its last domestic, conventional-format switcher. It was powered by a six-cylinder 251B engine and rated at 1,000 horsepower. Middletown & Hummelstown No. 1016 is among the last of the type in service, photographed at Middletown, Pennsylvania, on September 29, 2007. With the T-6, Alco revised its hood style and returned to the side-mounted radiators. The front of the hood features the gentle curves and notched number boards similar to those first used on the RSD-7 that were common to the RS-11 and other Alco road-switchers of the period. *Brian Solomon*

known for high-availability diesels, built respectable switchers. Switchers also usually had less taxing assignments. Where road diesels might work at maximum throttle for hours on end and received constant pounding from mainline duties, switchers only worked at maximum throttle for short periods and tended to rack up less mileage working in yards. While the lifespan of the early road diesels was about 15 years (rather less than that of unreliable models), diesel switchers worked for decades. Many switchers outlasted their manufacturers by a generation, and a few of the switchers bought during World War II are still working in as-built condition in 2009. That sort of endurance didn't leave room for a replacement market in the 1950s or 1960s.

Third, by the time switchers were due for replacement, their traditional work had largely dried up. Heavy industrial activity was in steep decline from 1960 onward, and thus so was the railroad's traditional carload business. Likewise, passenger services declined rapidly in this period and coach yards and passenger terminals that employed switchers were soon left with very little to switch. Even where passenger services survived, fixed consists and push-pull operations replaced traditional trains.

Last, railroads found that when they bought new road power, older road-switchers could be re-assigned to most switching duties. An RS-3 would work nearly as well switching as a new T-6.

RS-11

In February 1956, Alco introduced its latest four-motor road-switcher, the 1,800-horsepower model RS-11, specification DL701. It looked like a foreshortened version of the specialized high-horsepower RSD-7 introduced in 1954. Its tall, Spartan, and semi-streamlined hood design represented a departure from the RS-2/RS-3 that had been the mainstay of Alco's postwar production. The RS-11 was powered by the new 12-251B diesel—the first 251 engine in the V configuration. In addition to the new engine, Alco introduced an improved electrical system that featured fewer components, including relays, designed to ease maintenance and improve reliability.

Automatic motor transition was a standard feature. Motor transition serves a function for matching power characteristics similar to an automobile transmission gearbox. Various motor connection combinations were used to give optimum generator–traction motor characteristics for different rates of speed and output. Many early diesels, including most of Alco's initial postwar

The Maine Central bought a pair of RS-11s in 1956. Originally, No. 802 was painted for the railroad's Portland Terminal subsidiary, later transferred to the parent railroad. In February 1981, it displays a fresh coat of paint at the Waterville, Maine, shop. This locomotive tested briefly on Vermont's Green Mountain Railroad, working freight XR-1 from Bellows Falls to Rutland in late autumn 1983. *George S. Pitarys*

Opposite: Canadian National's Duluth, Winnipeg & Pacific subsidiary operated an unusual fleet of RS-11s with Canadian Dominion Foundries & Steel Company trucks and dynamic brakes. These were later transferred to CN's Central Vermont, where they worked in freight service until the mid-1980s. When the CV disposed of the fleet, most were picked up by short lines and locomotive leasing companies. On September 15, 1988, former DW&P No. 3604 works the Rochester & Southern's Brooks Avenue Yard in Rochester, New York. The locomotive is owned by Genesee Valley Transportation, which subsequently became a short-line operator in New York and Pennsylvania and acquired a substantial fleet of Alco diesels.
Brian Solomon

offerings, had been built with manual transition. When working the locomotive, the engineer initiated motor transitions by manually moving a transition lever in the cab. Forward transition was made as the locomotive gathered speed, and reverse transition was made as it slowed. Some engineers found that manual transition gave them a greater level of control over locomotive output, but the failure to initiate transitions at appropriate moments reduced locomotive efficiency and risked damage to equipment.

Alco built a three-unit RS-11 demonstrator set, which it sent on a 30,000-mile tour across the United States. Numbered 701, 701-A, and 701-B, these units were featured prominently in the trade press. *Railway Age* detailed the set's progress, highlighting various operational tests while noting its cleaner exhaust. The RS-11 was promoted as having distinct advantages over Alco's troubled RS-3. In true road-switcher tradition, demonstrator No. 701-B was steam generator–equipped so that it was capable of serving in passenger service. The units also featured Alco's new high-capacity dynamic brake equipment. The first RS-11 demo runs were on the Delaware & Hudson, which over the years had enjoyed the benefits of having Alco's plant along its main line. Working between Fort Edward and Saratoga Springs, New York, the 5,400-horsepower RS-11s hauled a freight weighing 4,863 tons. Climbing a 0.71-percent grade, they maintained a steady

On May 14, 1960, Toledo, Peoria & Western RS-11s Nos. 400 and 402 lead an eastward freight across the Illinois River at East Peoria, Illinois. The hood style associated with Alco's early 251 diesels was actually introduced with the 244-powered DL600 (RSD-7) in 1954, intended to make room for an improved dynamic braking system. The RS-11 was introduced two years later using a 251C rated at 1,800 horsepower. TP&W's three RS-11s were bought from Alco in 1958 and 1959, numbered 400 to 402.
C. Richard Neumiller

18 miles per hour with this tonnage. Working their way west, the RS-11s were tested on the Erie Railroad, where they hauled a 169-car freight weighing 7,280 tons in the flatlands of western Ohio and Indiana. No fewer than 11 test runs were performed on the Elgin, Joliet & Eastern. While in Chicago, a single RS-11 tested on U.S. Steel, demonstrating its ability to start 6,500 tons on wet rail, which *Railway Age* noted was accomplished without slipping. The RS-11s tested on the Milwaukee Road, Northern Pacific, and Spokane, Portland & Seattle (SP&S) before making a variety of tests on Southern Pacific (SP). On mountain grades in the West, Alco's RS-11 showed off its pulling ability, as well as its improved dynamic braking. Working the SP&S's Oregon Trunk, the RS-11s hauled a freight weighing an estimated 3,000 tons, notably starting on a 1.5-percent grade without slipping. On SP's Coast Line in California, the demos' dynamic brake held a 4,400-ton train to 20 miles per hour descending Cuesta Grade from Santa Margarita. SP also worked the steam generator–equipped unit in San Francisco–San Jose commute service (SP always called its peninsula suburban trains "commutes"). This passenger duty would prove to be rare work for the RS-11, which in service was largely a freight hauler.

VIA Rail FPA-4 No. 6770 leads the eastward *Atlantic* paused for a crew change and fuel, as well as adding water for the steam generators at Brownville Junction, Maine, on an icy night two days before Christmas 1980. VIA's *Atlantic* used a CP routing across Maine and, at the time, provided Maine's only scheduled passenger service. Built new, the 251-powered FPA-4 was unique to the Canadian market. *George S. Pitarys*

One of several Genesee Valley Transportation operations in New York state is the Falls Road Railroad, which operates former New York Central trackage between Lockport and Brockport, acquired from Conrail in 1996. RS-11 No. 1802 works sidings at Middleport, New York, on May 10, 2007. The locomotive was built in February 1959 for the Nickel Plate Road. It later served Norfolk & Western and Winchester & Western before GVT acquired it. *Brian Solomon*

Of the railroads that tested the RS-11, Delaware & Hudson, Northern Pacific, SP&S, and SP placed orders with Alco, while U.S. Steel acquired the 2,400 six-motor RSD-15s (discussed later in this chapter) for the Duluth, Missabe & Iron Range. Southern Pacific bought the demonstrators, followed by several orders for production RS-11s.

SP's final RS-11s were built with a low short hood and were among the earliest locomotives delivered with this innovation. Declining passenger services resulted in railroads requiring fewer locomotives with steam generators, so the space allocated for the equipment was unnecessary. Also, the mid-1950s saw the demise of the full carbody types, such as Alco's FA/FB, and road-switchers had become standard road power. Lowering the short hood, sometimes called the "nose," provided the crew with better forward visibility. Electro-Motive began offering its GP9 with a low-nose option about the same time as Alco. SP was a pioneer customer for both builders.

Another element of the hood arrangement related to the low-nose option was its operating orientation. The earlier Alco road-switchers emulated the running arrangement established by steam locomotives, and the long hood had generally been designated as the front. Most railroads' operating practice reflected this orientation, and engineers used to looking down the length of a boiler probably found gazing down the long hood familiar. On the RS-11, locomotive orientation was up to the ordering railroad, and as a result, the standard arrangement was effectively reversed. The short hood was often designated as the front—thus the interest in low short hoods. The

Toronto's Spedina Yard contains a host of Canadian National 251-powered MLWs on June 19, 1976. On the left is a pair of passenger-service FPA-4s; on the right are several RS-18s—MLW's equivalent to the RS-11. *Don Marson*

change in preference occurred fairly rapidly and, by the mid-1960s, short hood first with a low nose had become standard American practice. There were a few holdouts, notably Norfolk & Western, which was among the lines that continued to order locomotives long hood first with high short hoods as well.

Among the RS-11's strengths was its pulling power. Matt Wronski explains, "The RS-11 is a champ and it really digs in. These locomotives have good wheel slip [protection] and were weighted correctly. By comparison, Alco's later locomotives were more slippery on the rail."

The RS-11 became Alco's most prolific 251-powered model. Between 1956 and 1964, 426 were built for lines in the United States and Mexico. Louis A. Marre's *Diesel Locomotives: The First 50 Years* notes that domestic production ended in 1961, while MLW continued to build RS-11s for Mexican, but not Canadian, lines. Instead, MLW offered a Canadian variation, model RS-18, that used the hood style introduced with the 12-244-powered RS-10 (which didn't feature the notched nose) and employed a more traditional cab arrangement than the RS-11. Despite these minor external differences, under the hood, the RS-18 was nearly identical to the RS-11. RS-18s were sold exclusively in Canada; between 1956 and 1968, MLW built 351 of them. In later years, as Canadian lines thinned their rosters, some short lines acquired RS-18s for operation in the United States. Canadian Pacific routinely operated RS-18s on its American lines, and they were common on the Delaware & Hudson after CPR's acquisition of the line in 1990. The D&H, which had been the first to test Alco's 12-251 diesel, was also among the last to operate it on the main line.

RS-11 production ended when Alco introduced the RS-36, an 1,800-horsepower, four-motor road-switcher that appeared the same as the RS-11 externally, and even shared the DL701 specification, but benefited from solid-state electricals introduced on the RS-27 (discussed later in this chapter). The RS-36 remained in production for just two years and was discontinued in 1963, when the Century series was introduced. Alco built 40 RS-36s, many with the low short hood option.

SIX-MOTORS

Alco's 16-244 engine powered its DL600/DL600A, model RSD-7, introduced in 1954 and 1955. These were in production for just a few months before the DL600B, model RSD-15, with the more reliable 16-251B engine, supplanted it. Production total for the RSD-7 was just 17 units. The Santa Fe and Pennsylvania Railroad were the only customers. The RSD-15, which was

In the 1980s and 1990s, the Indiana Hi-Rail operated a regional network of disconnected lines. Indiana Hi-Rail RSD-15 No. 442 leads a northward empty grain train on the railroad's busiest line segment. Passing Griffin, Indiana, on December 27, 1991, the train is en route from Evansville, Indiana, to Browns, Illinois. Today, this Santa Fe RSD-15 is preserved in operable condition in Austin, Texas, by the Austin Steam Train Association and is painted in the old SP "Black Widow" freight livery. *Scott Muskopf*

Canadian National RS-18m 3153 leads a westward passenger train at Bayview Junction, Ontario, on June 18, 1976. In 1967, six CN's RS-18s were modified with head-end power generators and redesignated RS-18ms. They were dressed in orange and white and assigned to high-speed *Tempo* passenger services in Quebec and Ontario. *Don Marson*

virtually indistinguishable externally, sold more units. Like the DL600A, the DL600B was rated at 2,400 horsepower. While the original DL600 was rated at 2,250 horsepower, in its day this was considered very high output and was designed to compete with Fairbanks-Morse's Train-Master model H-24-66, built between 1953 and 1957. The four-year RSD-15 production run from 1956 to 1960 saw just 87 of the type built. MLW built a sole RSD-17 (specification DL624), which variously operated on Canadian Pacific, Canadian National, and Pacific Great Eastern. Built with a high short hood, this was lowered in later years. It worked on CPR in transfer service around Montreal into the mid-1990s.

Alco's RSD-7 and RSD-15 combined production just about equaled Fairbanks-Morse's domestic H-24-66 production. Relatively low production of these models has been attributed to low demand for high-output, six-motor types during this period. Yet, the types are intriguing because a decade later, high-horsepower six-motor diesels emerged as a standard type and, by the 1990s, completely dominated the road freight market in North America.

The Santa Fe made news in 1959 when it ordered RSD-15s with the low short hood variation. *Railway Age* noted that the Santa Fe assigned these 2,400-horsepower units to its Chicago–

Los Angeles road pool. At about the same time, the Santa Fe ordered Electro-Motive's equivalent SD24 with a low short hood for similar service. Southern Pacific, which tested the SD24, ordered Alco RSD-15s with low short hoods for its Cotton Belt subsidiary.

Alco also offered model RSD-12 (specification DL702), which was essentially a six-motor version of the RS-11. It was slightly longer and was powered by the 12-251B. It had a more powerful generator into order to supply six traction motors. Alco built 69 for domestic use and 92 for Mexico.

HIGH-HORSEPOWER FOUR-MOTORS

Always seeking ways to increase its market share, Alco tested the market in 1959 with a 2,400-horsepower four-motor diesel, the first B-B type with such a high output. Electro-Motive had introduced its 2,000-horsepower GP20 that year. When *Railway Age* emphasized the importance of Electro-Motive's adaptation of the turbocharger to the 16-567 to boost output, Alco's engineers were quick to point out that Alco had been using turbochargers for two decades. Yet, Alco's 2,400-horsepower DL640, model RS-27, attracted very little interest. Several Midwestern railroads sampled the RS-27, including the Chicago & North Western,

In summer 1963, Pennsylvania Railroad RSD-12s shove on the back of a westward freight ascending the famous Horseshoe Curve west of Altoona, Pennsylvania. The PRR sampled many of Alco's six-motor efforts. *Richard Jay Solomon*

Penn Central RS-27 No. 2402 works a cut of piggyback trailers at Rochester, New York, on March 10, 1974. Pennsylvania Railroad's 15 RS-27s, Nos. 2400 to 2414, represented the bulk of Alco's production. The 2,400-horsepower model was offered from late 1959 until it was superseded by the C-424, which used most of the same equipment. The RS-27's low-notched and unusually short front hood gave it a distinctive appearance. *Bill Dechau, Doug Eisele collection*

Green Bay & Western, and Soo Line. The PRR bought the bulk of production with 15 units. Coincidentally, the model number reflected total production. Perhaps Alco should have called it the RS-2400?

The RS-27 measured 57 feet, 2 1/2 inches long over couplers. Its mechanical and primary electrical components were essentially the same used on other 1950s-era 251 diesels, with the significant exception of the excitation system, which used solid-state components in place of traditional electricals. With an unusually short, notched, low short hood, the RS-27 was unlikely to be mistaken for any other diesel. Its essential configuration and proportions were later adopted by Alco's high-horsepower, four-motor Century models.

Concurrent with RS-27 production was the 2,000-horsepower RS-32, built in 1961 and 1962. Where the RS-27 was powered by the 16-251B, the RS-32 was powered by an uprated engine, the 12-cylinder model 251C. New York Central and Southern Pacific bought all 35 Alco RS-32s. The Central's were ordered for high-speed Flexivan intermodal service, but they didn't last too long on these assignments. Matt Wronski, who worked with the men that ran them, relates, "RS-32s were not well liked. They were slippery girls [referring to wheel slip] compared with the older Alcos, Central's FAs and RS-3s."

This 20-millimeter view accentuates the curves of the low nose on GVT RS-32 No. 2035, working on the Falls Road in 2008. In the course of four decades, the locomotive has worked for nine different railroads and is now back on the same tracks it plied for its original owner. It carries the number originally assigned to it as the result of Penn Central renumbering. All of the RS-32s were delivered with a low short hood, a feature introduced with the RSD-15.
Brian Solomon

The RS-32 was Alco's initial 2,000-horsepower four-motor road-switcher, introduced in 1961 to compete with Electro-Motive's GP20. Only New York Central and Southern Pacific bought it. GVT's No. 2035 was built as No. 8035, part of a 25-unit order for the Central, which classified the models as DRS-12s.
Brian Solomon

On July 20, 1965, a New York Central RS-32 leads an eastward freight along the Mohawk River near Amsterdam, New York. Central acquired 25 RS-32s in 1961–1962 for intermodal service. Crews found them slippery in comparison with older Alcos. *Jim Shaughnessy*

Privately owned Alco C-424 No. 4243 poses with the Adirondack Scenic Railroad excursion train at Lake Placid, New York, in October 2005. Built for Burlington Northern predecessor Spokane, Portland & Seattle, this C-424 had worked for a variety of owners, including the Massachusetts Central, where it served the 25-mile Ware River line in the mid-1990s. *Brian Solomon*

CENTURY SERIES

In 1963, Alco introduced its improved Century series in an effort to better its North American locomotive business. Where Alco had been struggling with sales in the 1950s, it faced increased competition on several fronts in the 1960s. Yet, it recognized that changes in tax laws and aging postwar diesels had opened up the domestic locomotive market for a period of mass sales potential. The Century was a marketing scheme aimed to demonstrate that Alco was still in the running and offering state-of-the-art locomotives.

When General Electric, Alco's one-time partner, officially entered the domestic locomotive market in 1960–1961 with its high-horsepower U25B, Alco knew it had a tough pull ahead. GE's

Right: A distinctive feature of the Century series was its angled front windows, designed to give crews a better view. A Delaware & Hudson brakeman boards C-628 No. 618 at Colonie, New York, in May 1969. *Jim Shaughnessy*

2,500-horsepower U25B was the most powerful locomotive on the American market. While in the 1950s high-horsepower locomotives had been largely ordered for specialty applications, by the early 1960s, American railroads were being sold on the concept of unit reduction, and three U25Bs could match the horsepower of five FA/FBs, RS-2/RS-3s, or Electro-Motive's standard F units rated at 1,500 horsepower.

Alco's Century incorporated a variety of minor improvements in an attractive new hood style. Many of the Century's refinements involved elements of its air systems. Notably, it featured a pressurized engine compartment, a concept pioneered by GE on the U25B and adopted a couple of years later by Electro-Motive with its GP30. In an effort to keep engine components cleaner by minimizing the accumulation of particulate matter and residual oil, interior air pressure was raised with exhaust from the main-generator cooling fan while the compartment was sealed from outside air. Traction motor ventilation was centralized, simplifying motor cooling equipment. The radiator arrangement was completely redesigned, with horizontally mounted radiator cores situated at the top of the hood at the back of the locomotive.

Lehigh Valley C-420 No. 409 leads westward freight JB-3 at East Victor, New York, on May 26, 1972. After the Lehigh Valley was folded into Conrail on April 1, 1976, all 12 of its C-420s were conveyed to the Delaware & Hudson. Eleven years later, these went to the Arkansas & Missouri, which retained some and sold others. While Nos. 409 and 415 were conveyed to the Indiana Hi-Rail and scrapped after many years in service, several other of the LV's attractive 2,000-horsepower road-switchers survive on short lines today. *Doug Eisele*

The Century's improved body design made it easier to remove primary components, which further reduced maintenance costs. Electrical innovations incorporated modern solid-state components to reduce the number of relays and traditional electrical gear. A new wheel slip protection system was designed for better traction and to allow smoother acceleration.

Unlike Alco's previous designations, the Century series models logically described powered axles and horsepower, similar to designations used by GE's Universal line. Each new Alco model used the C (for Century) followed by a three-digit number. The first digit indicated powered axles, the second and third represented approximate horsepower. Further simplifying matters, with the later Century models Alco organized specification numbers to closely resemble model designations.

Alco's 251 diesel powered its Century series. This 12-251C engine, destined for Lehigh Valley's C-420 No. 411, rests inside the company shops at Sayre, Pennsylvania, on February 27, 1972. *R. R. Richardson, Doug Eisele collection*

In the 1980s, VIA Rail bought F40PHs and disposed of many of its FPA-4s inherited from Canadian National and Canadian Pacific. California's Napa Valley Wine Train began excursion service in autumn 1989 using former Rio Grande Ski Train heavyweight cars and former VIA Rail FPA-4s. Although railroads in the United States didn't buy new 251-powered carbody units in the 1950s, former VIA Rail units found homes on a variety of American short lines and tourist railways. *Brian Solomon*

Arizona's Apache Railway works four immaculately maintained Alco C-420s west of Snowflake on September 11, 1991. The Apache is a short line that has collected a variety of Alco and MLW diesels for service on its 38-mile line between its interchange with the former Santa Fe at Holbrook and Snowflake. Three of its four C-420s, Nos. 81 to 83, were former Louisville & Nashville units. The remaining unit, No. 84, is formerly of Norfolk & Western. In 1998, the Apache acquired some former CP Rail C-424s, allowing it to retire its three RS-36s, which it had bought new from Alco in the early 1960s. *C. Richard Neumiller*

The Belt Railway of Chicago operated a small fleet of C-424s bought new from Alco in 1966. These worked transfer runs and local freights on the railroad's freight-intensive Chicago terminal network. This photo provides a detailed view of the cab of BRC No. 602 on July 2, 1995. The BRC disposed of its Centuries in 1999, and most survive on various North American short lines. *Brian Solomon*

New York's Livonia, Avon & Lakeville is an all-Alco railroad that began operations on former Erie Railroad trackage between Avon and Lakeville in 1964. In 1996, it greatly expanded operations with the acquisition of lines from Conrail. On October 26, 1987, nearly a decade before expansion, LA&L C-425 No. 425 and RS-1 No. 20 switch corn syrup traffic at Lakeville after having run to Avon to collect 38 cars of interchange from Conrail. The LA&L keeps its working Alcos in exceptionally good condition. No. 425 was originally New Haven No. 2557 and was acquired from Conrail in 1981. *Brian Solomon*

FOUR-MOTOR CENTURIES

The first two four-axle Century models, C-420 and C-424, were effectively upgraded versions of the RS-32 and RS-27. Like the RS-32, the C-420 used a 12-cylinder 251B generating 2,000 horsepower, but it measured 60 feet, 3 inches long, making it slightly longer. The C-420 was identifiable by its longer front hood. It was built exclusively for the American market between 1963 and 1968 and was ordered in both low-nose and high-nose variations. Two railroads, the Long Island Rail Road and Monon, bought high-nose versions for passenger services.

The C-424 used a 16-cylinder 251B generating 2,400 horsepower. It was built in both the United States and Canada. In 1964, on the request of the Erie Lackawanna, Alco boosted output of the C-424 by 100 horsepower to match GE's 2,500-horsepower U25B. The new locomotive model, C-425, used the uprated 16-cylinder 251C engine, which obtained additional horsepower through a slightly faster maximum speed than the 251B and other minor modifications. The

Arkansas & Missouri C-420 No. 58 and RS-32 No. 42 reveal the stylistic change introduced with the Century series. The C-420 essentially replaced the RS-32 in Alco's catalog. Both locomotives are powered by 12-251C engines rated at 2,000 horsepower. Notice the brass bells shining in the evening sun mounted near the number boards. These bells are an A&M trademark and are hand-polished every day before the locomotives go out on the road. *Tom Kline*

No fewer than seven Alco diesels lead Arkansas & Missouri's daily Monett Turn southward on April 8, 2004. In the lead is C-420 No. 64. The town of Seligman, Missouri, in the background was once a connection with the Missouri & Arkansas Railway—later the Arkansas & Ozarks short line. Today, the A&M is one of the few remaining lines to routinely operate Alcos in multiple in road freight service. *Scott Muskopf*

The Long Island Rail Road was unusual for the fleet of high-hood C-420s it operated in commuter service. In June 1970, No. 214, running long hood forward, leads an eastward LIRR train at Union Hall, Long Island. Much of the LIRR is electrified with direct current third rail, and diesel-powered trains serve routes beyond electrified territory. *George W. Kowanski*

Erie Lackawanna was one of six railroads to purchase this model. A total of 190 C-424s (53 to railroads in the United States) were built by Alco and MLW, and 91 Alco C-425s compared with 476 General Electric U25Bs. Although not as prolific as the U25Bs, Alco's C-424s and C-425s have had much longer service lives. Most U25Bs were retired by 1980, although a few lasted into the mid-1980s. Many Alco and MLW Centuries toiled well into the 1990s, and a surprising number of four-axle Century locomotives are still working for short line carriers more than 40 years after they were built.

In an attempt to match Electro-Motive's 3,000-horsepower GP40—the first of its new 645 engine–equipped diesels introduced in 1965 and 1966—Alco introduced its equivalent C-430. It featured the same variant of the 251 and related electrical changes introduced on the C-630 described later in this chapter. Just 16 C-430s were built, 10 purchased by long-time Alco stalwart New York Central, assigned to fast freight service on its Water Level Route, including Flexivan intermodal trains. Among the features offered on the Central's C-430 were

On March 3, 1968, Toledo, Peoria & Western C-424 No. 800 rests at East Peoria, Illinois. Considering its relatively small locomotive fleet, the T&PW operated a variety of Alco diesels, including seven RS-2s, one RS-3, three RS-11s, and two C-424s, Nos. 800 and 801. These last two were built in September 1964 and were sold in the 1980s to the Morristown & Erie, where they have continued to work for more than two decades. *C. Richard Neumiller*

Lashing rain leaves a shiny gloss on the Delaware-Lackawanna's tracks and yard office at South Scranton, Pennsylvania. Genesee Valley Transportation's D-L has amassed a substantial fleet of Alcos acquired from myriad sources and of many lineages. C-425 No. 2456 wears British Columbia Railroad paint, a line where it labored for several decades. It was built as Erie Lackawanna No. 2456 in 1964. GVT's dedicated mechanics keep its Alcos in regular service.
Brian Solomon

On October 13, 2005, more than 29 years after the Erie Lackawanna was melded into Conrail, former EL C-425 No. 2461 leads Delaware-Lackawanna freight PT97 in a heavy autumn rain at Slateford Junction, Pennsylvania, on the former Lackawanna main line. The D-L is a short line operated by Genesee Valley Transportation, which operates several former Conrail and Delaware & Hudson line segments in New York and Pennsylvania, using one of the most significant remaining fleets of Alco diesels in the United States.
Brian Solomon

On request of the Erie Lackawanna, Alco boosted output of the C-424 to 2,500 horsepower, resulting in the C-425 model. EL C-425 No. 2462 leads a quartet of Alco Centuries at Hepburn, Ohio, on March 28, 1976, three days before Conrail assumed operation of the Erie Lackawanna and other bankrupt Eastern railroads. No. 2462 was one of 12 EL C-425s acquired by the BC Rail in April 1976. While this one was scrapped in 1990, six others were acquired from the BCR by Genesee Valley Transportation, where several remain in service. *Bill Dechau, Doug Eisele collection*

This detail of the rear hood, headlight, and number boards of Delaware-Lackawanna No. 2461 was taken at Scranton, Pennsylvania, in September 2007. This locomotive has been painted in a livery similar to that used by the Erie Lackawanna in its later years.
Brian Solomon

Alco's C-430 demonstrators operate with its dynamometer car (acquired from the Nickel Plate Road) on a Delaware & Hudson freight at Colonie, New York, on April 1, 1967. Alco's most powerful four-motor diesel had few buyers. Yet, like many of Alco's later diesels, the few that were built generally enjoyed long working lives. Several are still active in 2009. *Jim Shaughnessy*

Alco's four-motor "Hi-Ad" high-adhesion trucks, although models were also built with Alco's conventional trucks.

In 1966, Alco introduced the C-415, billed as a utility locomotive. This center-cab switcher was built with both normal and high-profile cabs and was powered by an eight-cylinder 251E engine. This model also offered the Hi-Ad trucks, although only a few were built with them. The C-415 was not well received and only 26 were built, compared with more than 800 EMD SW1500s produced at about the same time for essentially the same type of service.

BIG CENTURIES

Big high-horsepower locomotives caught the attention of America's railroads in the early 1960s. When the Century was introduced, it wasn't clear how locomotives would evolve, so Alco kept its options open. To understand why Alco engineered a variety of unusual models, it is necessary to study the offerings of its competitors. GE's U25B had set a new standard for high-horsepower four-motors, while German diesel builder Krauss-Maffei was entertaining Southern Pacific and Rio Grande with super high–horsepower diesel hydraulics (these used a torque-converter hydraulic transmission in place of an electric transmission).

One of the more unusual Century models was this 1,500-horsepower C-415. No. 701 works at Burlington, Iowa, on the Burlington Junction Railway on October 10, 2000. This is one of two C-415s used by the line. No. 701 was among the last Alcos built by Schenectady and was delivered to Washington logging railroad Columbia & Cowlitz in late 1968. It features the high cab and Alco's unusual late-era Hi-Ad B trucks. The C&C traded an F-M road-switcher to Alco as part of the order. *Terry Norton*

Both Electro-Motive and GE had introduced double-diesels in September 1963. These were essentially two four-motor types under one hood. Where Electro-Motive used four-axle trucks, GE adopted the B-B+B-B arrangement it had used on some electrics and its 1950s-era turbines for Union Pacific. Initially, Electro-Motive only offered its DD35 as a cabless B-unit, designed to run with its 2,500-horsepower GP35s. Both builders interested Union Pacific and Southern Pacific, which were the two prime customers for super-powerful diesels.

In spring 1964, Alco offered its version of the double-diesel by constructing a unique A-B-A set of eight-axle C-855s for use by Union Pacific. This was a short-lived attempt to enter the eight-motor, double-diesel market. Like GE, Alco employed the B-B+B-B arrangement. Each of the three units was rated at 5,500 horsepower, powered by dual 16-251C engines. Intending to compete with Krauss-Maffei, Alco licensed the Voith hydraulic torque converter and, in 1964, built three 4,300-horsepower six-axle diesel-hydraulics powered by dual 12-251Cs. These were lettered for SP. No further orders were made, and the locomotives remained an odd curiosity. Although for a few years SP operated a significant fleet of German D-H locomotives, maintenance costs ultimately put a damper on future development of this type in the United States.

All three locomotive manufacturers built massive double-diesels for Union Pacific in the 1960s. Alco's effort was this A-B-A set of C-855s, each unit riding on four pairs of B trucks and powered by dual 16-251 engines. They were 86 feet long, weighed 528,000 pounds, and were slightly taller than typical Century models. *Jay Williams collection*

In 1979, Delaware & Hudson painted its C-628s a minimalist blue with yellow striping immediately prior to shipping the locomotives to Mexico. No. 605 is pictured at the Colonie Shops on May 10, 1979. *Jim Shaughnessy*

Far more successful than Alco's dabbling in double-diesel and hydraulic technology was further development of more conventional, single-engine, six-motor diesel-electrics. Although Alco had offered a variety of six-motor types in the 1950s, these were largely ordered for specialized applications. The Santa Fe and SP's interest in the RSD-15 in the late 1950s hinted at future interest. Yet, where the double-diesels and hydraulic types only generated select interest from big Western roads, the six-motor diesel-electric found applications across North America. When it introduced the Century series, Alco initially offered an improved version of the RSD-15, tentatively designated C-624. This would have blended all the essential characteristics of the RSD-15 with the Century improvements, but it was never built. Instead, Alco refined its six-motor design and introduced the 2,750-horsepower C-628 in late 1963, a model Alco billed as the most powerful single-engine diesel-electric in North America—a title it held for a few years.

The C-628 was longer than the RSD-15, measuring 69 feet between couplers (later figures indicate 69 feet, 6 inches). It was powered by the uprated 16-cylinder 251C engine. To match the output of the engine, it used the slightly more powerful GT-586A4 main generator and six GE-752E6A traction motors. While the 752 motor had been in production since the late 1940s, improvements in insulating materials had gradually enabled GE to engineer increasingly more robust designs. These improvements, combined with other GE electrical innovations, contributed to the more powerful locomotive designs offered by both GE and Alco in the 1960s. The C-628 was offered with 74:18 and 80:23 gearing, although all the domestic units used the 74:18 ratio. As with Alco's earlier commercial six-motors, the C-628 rode on tri-mount trucks. This feature brought many complaints, both from crews, who disliked the poor ride quality, and from railroads, which were unhappy with excessive track wear.

A total of 186 units were built during the C-628's five-year production run at Schenectady; 135 of them went to domestic railroads. The remaining units were sold to lines in Mexico and Australia. The Atlantic Coast Line was first to acquire C-628s with an order for four in December 1963. The C-628 was built in several variations. Most unusual were Norfolk & Western's, which also represented the largest domestic fleet. N&W placed orders in 1965 and 1966 for 30 locomotives. All came with dual controls (two complete sets of engineer's controls that made bi-directional operation easier) with the long hood designated as the front, and with high short hoods. Although unique for the C-628, this was a typical N&W arrangement for new diesels. In the mid-1970s, N&W sold its C-628s to the Chicago & North Western, which operated them for another decade based out of Escanaba, Michigan.

Alco supplemented the C-628 in 1965 with the introduction of its more powerful C-630. This featured several significant technological innovations, notably an AC-DC transmission system made possible by advances in silicon diode solid-state technology—the first of its kind in the United States. As inferred by its designation, the C-630 was rated at 3,000 horsepower. This 251E engine received modifications that included raising maximum speed to 1,100 rpm and altering the manifold. Although Schenectady's production of the C-630 ceased in 1968, MLW

Opposite: Penn Central C-628 No. 6300 shows off a fresh coat of paint at Goodman Street Yard in Rochester, New York, on June 28, 1970. The shiny appearance of the PC Alco is ironic because this photo was taken less than a year and a half after Alco ended locomotive production and just a week after Penn Central declared bankruptcy. *Doug Eisele*

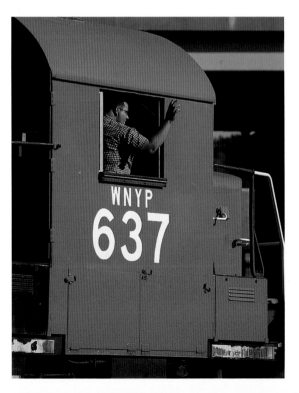

Above: Chicago & North Western bought Norfolk & Western's unique high-hood C-628s in the 1970s and assigned them to Escanaba for ore-train services in the Upper Peninsula of Michigan, as well as this manifest freight to Chicago. A pair of the unusual six-motors works a freight toward Green Bay at Nadeau, Michigan, on July 10, 1980. *Terry Norton*

Right: Western New York & Pennsylvania engineer Chris Southwell gives a friendly wave from the cab of a former Cartier M-636 at Meadville, Pennsylvania. For years, the old Erie was a large purchaser of Alco products. Today, this short line operates portions of the Erie and remains one of the last bastions for big Alco/MLW diesels in road service. *Brian Solomon*

continued to build its variation, designated M-630, until 1972. The AC-DC transmission was a significant innovation, soon adopted by both Electro-Motive and GE, which ultimately made greater commercial use of it than Alco. Combined, Alco and MLW sold 200 C-630/M-630s (including units to Mexico). It was one of Alco's most successful six-motor designs, yet it faired poorly in comparison to Electro-Motive's SD40 at 1,200 units, and GE's U30C at 600 units.

In 1967, two years after Electro-Motive brought out the 3,600-horsepower SD45, Alco introduced its final six-motor design, the 3,600-horsepower C-636. While Electro-Motive achieved a 3,600-horsepower engine by increasing the number cylinders from 16 to 20, Alco chose another path. To boost the output of its 251 prime mover by 20 percent required a variety of technical modifications. Richard T. Steinbrenner, in his *The American Locomotive Company: A Centennial Remembrance*, detailed the changes that resulted in the 16-251F engine, which included sophisticated adjustments to the camshaft and its timing, increasing the valve overlap to allow for greater power without increasing operating temperatures in the major engine systems. A new turbocharger was designed that forced air into the cylinders at higher pressure. Pistons were redesigned to incorporate a steel cap and improved flow of cooling oil. There were additional changes to fuel injection pumps and a slight change to the crankcase. Engine speed was the same as the 251E, producing maximum power at 1,100 rpm. The higher-output engine required greater radiator capacity and an improved cooling system. The six-motor Hi-Ad truck, which had been an option with the C-630, was offered as a standard feature with the C-636. Using 81:22 gearing with 40-inch wheels, the C-636 developed 100,000 pounds maximum continuous tractive effort at 7 miles per hour, and maximum speed was 75 miles per hour.

Ore-hauling Cartier Railway, which operated 260 miles of railroad between Port Cartier, Quebec, and Mont Wright, had one of the last large fleets of six-motor Alco/MLW diesels in North America working in daily service. Cartier M-636 No. 82 leads a southward loaded train near Dog siding in the Sept Iles National Park, 49 miles from the docks at Port Cartier. Long sections of the railway are completely inaccessible by paved road, which requires the use of helicopters to transport crews. An order for six-motor General Electric diesels in 2001 ended Alco/MLW supremacy on this isolated line. *Brian Solomon*

Minnesota iron ore hauler Erie Mining C-424 No. 7230 works with RS-11 No. 7216 at Hoyt Lakes on November 30, 1990, moving a train of dump cars. In later years, this railroad was operated by LTV Mining, best known for its surviving fleet of Electro-Motive F9s. Its Alco fleet consisted of 17 RS-11s (15 purchased new by Erie Mining, 2 acquired secondhand) along with 3 C-420s and this lone C-424. *John Leopard*

The innovations didn't buy Alco much time; the C-636 remained in American production for less than a year, selling just 34 units to four customers. The largest order for C-636s was made by Pennsylvania Railroad, which vanished into the Penn Central while the locomotives were in production; the locomotives were delivered to the PC dressed in a somber black and adorned with the Penn Central "mating worms" logo.

The Canadian version, model M-636, was more successful and marketed by MLW until 1975, representing an additional 100 locomotives. In the United States, the C-636 survived for little more than a decade, but in Canada a number of C-636s and M-636s worked well into the 1990s. One of the last significant fleets for the type was on the isolated Quebec Cartier ore-hauling line in northern Quebec. Here, they received excellent maintenance and worked in daily heavy-haul service, moving 14,000-ton iron-ore trains until being replaced by modern General Electric AC-traction diesels in 2001–2002. These locomotives were well cared for by the Cartier's maintenance forces, and a few have continued to serve on American short lines into 2009.

END OF THE LINE

Alco's 251 design had largely overcome the failings of the 244 engine. The Century line was a good product and inspired equivalent locomotives offered by Alco's competitors. Despite innovation, Alco had an increasingly difficult time selling its locomotives. In the six years that Alco's Century line was produced at Schenectady, which covered more than eight models, it accounted for fewer than 700 units (including 91 locomotives built for lines in Mexico). For comparison, Schenectady had built more than 1,200 RS-3s in the same span of time between 1950 and 1956, and the RS-3 represented only a portion of its domestic production at the time.

Former LIRR No. 213 is a long way from Long Island. It was a warm evening on May 29, 1995, when old 213 worked with an SD7 on Dakota Southern's former Milwaukee Road line near Kimball, South Dakota. Both locomotives are painted in a livery reminiscent of the former Rock Island. *Brian Solomon*

Years after six-motor Alcos had faded from favor in the United States, they remained in road service in Canada. On October 12, 1980, Canadian National six-motor MLWs catch the sun at Gordon Yard in Moncton, New Brunswick. For many years, Gordon supported CN's locomotive fleet assigned to the Maritime Provinces. Into the 1980s, it was an MLW stronghold, where General Motors products were the exception rather the rule. *Don Marson*

Setting into thick New Jersey smog, the sun makes for a colorful silhouette of a Central Railroad of New Jersey RS-3 and a heavyweight passenger car in May 1966. *Richard Jay Solomon*

As a minority builder with marginal resources, Alco faced an uphill struggle to keep pace with changes in the market. Albert J. Churella explains that Alco was never able to make up time it had lost during World War II period, and General Motors had effectively redefined the locomotive business and emerged as the market leader. As Alco weakened, it suffered from the perception that it might exit the market, and that made many railroads hesitant to invest too heavily in its locomotives. During the 1960s, its situation worsened; Alco continued to lose market share, not just to General Motors' Electro-Motive Division, but also to its one-time partner, General Electric.

In the late 1950s, as the only domestic competitor to General Motors' Electro-Motive Division, Alco was more or less assured a portion of the market so long as it could offer an equivalent product. When GE began competing for market share, the scales were tipped against Alco. It now had to vie for sales against two giant companies. Furthermore, it was in the awkward position of having to rely upon a competitor for its electrical components. This put Alco at a twofold disadvantage: It faced an obvious cost disadvantage versus GE locomotives, and yet it was largely subservient to GE for electrical innovation. General Motors had been producing its own electrical gear since the late 1930s, so it didn't face these problems.

The Worthington Corporation, a conglomerate that produced a variety of industrial products, purchased Alco in 1964. Initially, this change in ownership had little effect on Alco's ability to market its locomotives. Its sales continued to slip, however, and after more than two decades of difficulties, Alco exited the new-locomotive market in 1969.

But this was not the end of the story. Alco continued to supply parts, while its MLW affiliate licensed Alco's designs and continued to construct new locomotives into the mid-1970s. Bombardier bought the Alco licenses from MLW in the mid-1970s and continued to build the locomotives until the mid-1980s.

SOURCES

BOOKS

Alexander, Edwin P. *American Locomotives: A Pictorial Record of SteamPower*. New York: Bonanza, 1950.

Alymer-Small, Sidney. *The Art of Railroading, Vol. VIII*. Chicago: Railway Publications Society, 1908.

American Railroad Journal, 1966. San Marino, Calif.: Golden West Books. 1966.

Archer, Robert F. *The History of the Lehigh Valley Railroad: The Route of the Black Diamond*. Berkeley, Calif.: Howell-North, 1977.

Armstrong, John H. *The Railroad: What It Is, What It Does*. Omaha, Neb.: Simmons-Boardman, 1982.

Bruce, Alfred W. *The Steam Locomotive in America: Its Development in the Twentieth Century*. New York: Norton, 1952.

Bush, Donald J. *The Streamlined Decade*. New York: Braziller, 1975.

Casey, Robert J., and W. A. S. Douglas. *The Lackawanna Story: The First Hundred Years of the Delaware, Lackawanna and Western Railroad*. New York: McGraw-Hill, 1951.

Churella, Albert J. *From Steam to Diesel: Managerial Customs and Organizational Capabilities in the Twentieth-Century American Locomotive Industry*. Princeton, N.J.: Princeton University Press, 1998.

Conrad, J. David. *The Steam Locomotive Directory of North America, Vol. I*. Polo, Ill.: Transportation Trails, 1988.

———.*The Steam Locomotive Directory of North America, Vol. II*. Polo, Ill.: Transportation Trails, 1988.

Delaware and Hudson Company. *A Century of Progress: History of the Delaware and Hudson Company, 1823–1923*. Albany, N.Y.: Lyon, 1925.

Dixon, Thomas W. Jr. *Chesapeake & Ohio: Superpower to Diesels*. Newton, N.J.: Walthers, 1984.

Doherty, Timothy Scott, and Brian Solomon. *Conrail*. St. Paul, Minn.: MBI Publishing Company, 2004.

Dolzall, Gary W., and Stephen F. Dolzall. *Diesels from Eddystone: The Story of Baldwin Diesel Locomotives*. Milwaukee, Wis.: Kalmbach, 1984.

———. *Monon: The Hoosier Line*. Glendale, Calif.: Interurban Press, 1987.

Draney, John. *Diesel Locomotives—Electrical Equipment: A Practical Treatise on the Operation and Maintenance of Railway Diesel Locomotives*. Chicago: American Technical Society, 1949.

Drury, George H. *Guide to North American Steam Locomotives*. Waukesha, Wis.: Kalmbach, 1993.

Dunscomb, Guy L. *A Century of Southern Pacific Steam Locomotives, 1862–1962*. Modesto, Calif.: Dunscomb, 1963.

Farrington, S. Kip Jr. *Railroading from the Head End*. New York: Doubleday, Doran & Company, 1943.

———. *Railroads at War*. New York: Coward-McCann, 1944.

———. *Railroading from the Rear End*. New York: Coward-McCann, 1946.

———. *Railroading the Modern Way*. New York: Coward-McCann, 1951.

Forney, M. N. *Catechism of the Locomotive*. New York: Railroad Gazette, 1876.

Garmany, John B. *Southern Pacific Dieselization*. Edmonds, Wash.: Pacific Fast Mail, 1985.

Harlow, Alvin F. *The Road of the Century: The Story of the New York Central*. New York: Creative Age Press, 1947.

Hartley, Scott. *New England Alcos in Twilight*. Homewood, Ill.: Pentrex, 1984.

Hungerford, Edward. *Men of Erie: A Story of Human Effort*. New York: Random House, 1946.

Jones, Robert Willoughby. *Boston and Albany: The New York Central in New England, Vol. 1*. Los Angeles: Pine Tree Press, 1997.

———. *Boston and Albany: The New York Central in New England, Vol. 2*. Los Angeles: Pine Tree Press, 2000.

Keilty, Edmund. *Interurbans without Wires: The Rail Motorcar in the United States*. Glendale, Calif.: Interurban Press, 1979.

Kiefer, P. W. *A Practical Evaluation of Railroad Motive Power*. New York: Simmons-Boardman, 1948.

Kirkland, John F. *Dawn of the Diesel Age: The History of the Diesel Locomotive in America*. Pasadena, Calif.: Interurban Press, 1983.

———. *The Diesel Builders, Vol .1: Fairbanks-Morse and Lima-Hamilton*. Glendale, Calif.: Interurban Press, 1985.

———. *The Diesel Builders, Vol. 2: American Locomotive Company and Montreal Locomotive Works*. Glendale, Calif.: Interurban Press, 1989.

———. *The Diesel Builders, Vol. 3: Baldwin Locomotive Works*. Glendale, Calif.: Interurban Press, 1994.

Klein, Maury. *Union Pacific: Vol. 1*. Minneapolis: University of Minnesota Press, 2006.

———. *Union Pacific: Vol. 2*. Minneapolis: University of Minnesota Press, 2006.

Kratville, William W., and Harold E. Ranks. *Motive Power of the Union Pacific*. Omaha, Neb.: Barnhart Press, 1958.

Marre, Louis A. *Diesel Locomotives: The First 50 Years: A Guide to Diesels Built Before 1972*. Waukesha, Wis.: Kalmbach, 1995.

Marre, Louis A., and Jerry A. Pinkepank. *The Contemporary Diesel Spotter's Guide*. Milwaukee, Wis.: Kalmbach, 1985.

McDonald, Charles W., and George H. Drury. *Diesel Locomotive Rosters: United States, Canada, Mexico*. Milwaukee, Wis.: Kalmbach, 1982.

McDonnell, Greg. *U-Boats: General Electric's Diesel Locomotives*. Toronto: Stoddart, 1994.

McMillan, Joe. *Santa Fe's Diesel Fleet*. Burlingame, Calif.: Chatham, 1975.

Middleton, William D. *When the Steam Railroads Electrified*. Milwaukee, Wis.: Kalmbach, 1974.

Morgan, David P. *Steam's Finest Hour*. Milwaukee, Wis.: Kalmbach, 1959.

Nowak, Ed, and Karl R. Zimmermann. *Ed Nowak's New York Central: A Company Photographer's View of the Railroad, 1941–1967*. Park Forest, Ill.: PTJ Publishing, 1983.

Pinkepank, Jerry A. *The Diesel Spotter's Guide*. Milwaukee, Wis.: Kalmbach, 1967.

———. *The Second Diesel Spotter's Guide*. Milwaukee, Wis.: Kalmbach, 1973.

Ransome-Wallis, P. *World Railway Locomotives: The Concise Encyclopedia*. New York: Hutchinson, 1959.

Reagan, H. C. Jr. *Locomotive Mechanism and Engineering*. New York: Wiley, 1894.

Reck, Franklin M. *On Time: The History of Electro-Motive Division of General Motors Corporation*. La Grange, Ill.: Electro-Motive Division of General Motors, 1948.

———. *The Dilworth Story: The Biography of Richard Dilworth, Pioneer Developer of the Diesel Locomotive*. New York: McGraw-Hill, 1954.

Reich, Sy. *Diesel Locomotive Rosters: The Railroad Magazine Series*. New York: Wayner, 1973.

Rose, Joseph R. *American Wartime Transportation*. New York: Crowell, 1953.

Saunders, Richard, Jr. *The Railroad Mergers and the Coming of Conrail*. Westport, Conn.: Greenwood Press, 1978.

——. *Merging Lines: American Railroads, 1900–1970*. DeKalb, Ill.: Northern Illinois University Press, 2001.

Shaughnessy, Jim. *Delaware & Hudson: The History of an Important Railroad whose Antecedent Was a Canal Network to Transport Coal*. Berkeley, Calif.: Howell-North, 1967.

Shuster, Philip, with Eugene L. Huddleston and Alvin F. Staufer. *C&O Power: Steam and Diesel Locomotives of the Chesapeake and Ohio Railway, 1900–1965*. Carrollton, Ohio: Staufer, 1965.

Signor, John R. *Tehachapi: Southern Pacific–Santa Fe*. San Marino, Calif.: Golden West, 1983.

——. *Donner Pass: Southern Pacific's Sierra Crossing*. San Marino, Calif.: Golden West, 1985.

Sinclair, Angus. *Development of the Locomotive Engine*. New York: D. VanNostrand, 1907.

Smith, Warren L. *Berkshire Days on the Boston & Albany: The Steam Locomotives of the B&A, 1925–1950*. New York: Quadrant Press, 1982.

Solomon, Brian. *The American Steam Locomotive*. Osceola, Wis.: MBI Publishing Company, 1998.

——. *Trains of the Old West*. New York: MetroBooks, 1998.

——. *The American Diesel Locomotive*. Osceola, Wis.: MBI Publishing Company, 2000.

——. *Super Steam Locomotives*. Osceola, Wis.: MBI Publishing Company, 2000.

——. *Locomotive*. St. Paul, Minn.: MBI Publishing Company, 2001.

——. *Railway Masterpieces: Celebrating the World's Greatest Trains, Stations and Feats of Engineering*. Iola, Wis.: Krause, 2002.

——. *GE Locomotives*. St. Paul, Minn.: MBI Publishing Company, 2003.

——. *Burlington Northern Santa Fe Railway*. St. Paul, Minn.: MBI Publishing Company, 2005.

——. *CSX*. St. Paul, Minn.: MBI Publishing Company, 2005.

——. *EMD Locomotives*. St. Paul, Minn.: Voyageur Press, 2006.

Solomon, Brian, and Mike Schafer. *New York Central Railroad*. Osceola, Wis.: MBI Publishing Company, 1999.

Staff, Virgil. *D-Day on the Western Pacific: A Railroad's Decision to Dieselize*. Glendale, Calif.: Interurban Press, 1982.

Staufer, Alvin F. *Steam Power of the New York Central System, 1915–1955*. Medina, Ohio: Staufer Books, 1961.

——. *New York Central's Early Power, 1831–1916*. Medina, Ohio: Staufer, 1967.

——. *Pennsy Power III: Steam, Electric, MU's, Motor Cars, Diesel Cars, Buses, Trucks, Airplanes, Boats, Art, 1847–1968*. Medina, Ohio: Staufer, 1993.

Staufer, Alvin F. and Edward L. May. *New York Central's Later Power, 1910–1968*. Medina, Ohio: Wayner, 1981.

Steinbrenner, Richard T., Bill J. Battle, Ernest E. Johnson, and Theodore F. Steinbrenner. *The American Locomotive Company: A Centennial Remembrance*. Warren, N.J.: On Track Publishers, 2003.

Strapac, Joseph A. *Southern Pacific Motive Power Annual 1971*. Burlingame, Calif.: Chatham, 1971.

——. *Southern Pacific Review 1981*. Huntington Beach, Calif.: Pacific Coast Chapter of the Railway and Locomotive Historical Society, 1982.

——. *Southern Pacific Review 1953–1985*. Huntington Beach, Calif.: Railway & Locomotive Historical Society, 1986.

Swengel, Frank M. *The American Steam Locomotive: Vol. 1, Evolution*. Davenport, Iowa: Midwest Rails Publications, 1967.

Taber, Thomas Townsend. *The Delaware, Lackawanna & Western Railroad, the Road of Anthracite*. Muncy, Pa.: Taber, 1977.

——. *The Delaware, Lackawanna & Western Railroad in the Nineteenth Century, 1828–1899*. Muncy, Pa.: Taber, 1977.

White, John H., Jr. *Early American Locomotives: With 147 Engravings*. New York: Courier Dover Publications, 1972.

——. *A History of the American Locomotive: Its Development, 1830–1880*. New York: Courier Dover Publications, 1979.

Williams, Harold A. *The Western Maryland Railway Story: A Chronicle of the First Century, 1852–1952*. Baltimore, Md.: Western Maryland Railway Company, 1952.

BROCHURES, RULEBOOKS, AND TIMETABLES

American Locomotive Company. *Louisiana Purchase Exposition*. New York, 1904.

American Locomotive Company and General Electric Corporation. *Operating Manual Model RS-3*. Schenectady, N.Y., 1951.

Alco-Méditerranée S.A.R.L. *Alco 251 Diesels*. Paris (no date).

Central Vermont Railway. *Timetable 65, Northern and Southern Division*. 1965.

Proceedings of the Institution of Mechanical Engineers. *Diesel Locomotives for the Future*. New York, 1987.

Seaboard Coast Line Railroad Company. *Instructions and Information Pertaining to Diesel Electric Engines*. Jacksonville, Fla., 1972.

PERIODICALS

Baldwin Locomotives. Philadelphia: Baldwin Locomotive Works. [no longer published]

CTC Board. Ferndale, Wash.

Diesel Era. Halifax, Pa.

Diesel Railway Traction (supplement to Railway Gazette, U.K.). [merged into Railway Gazette]

Extra 2200 South. Cincinnati.

Jane's World Railways. London.

Modern Railways. Surrey, U.K.

Official Guide to the Railways (1869 to 1995). New York.

Pacific RailNews. Waukesha, Wis. [no longer published]

Passenger Train Journal. Waukesha, Wis. [no longer published]

Railroad History. Boston. [formerly Railway and Locomotive Historical Society Bulletin]

Railway Age. Chicago and New York.

Railway and Locomotive Engineering. [no longer published]

Railway Mechanical Engineer (1925–1952). New York [no longer published]

Shoreliner. Grafton, Mass.

Trains Magazine. Waukesha, Wis.

Vintage Rails. Waukesha, Wis. [no longer published]

INDEX